W9-BDB-034

NO - - '14
w9/14

TEENAGERS 101

PROPERTY OF C L P L

Rebecca Deurlein, Ed.D.

Teenagers 101

What a Top Teacher Wishes You Knew About Helping Your Kid Succeed

ꞬAMACOM
American Management Association

New York | Atlanta | Brussels | Chicago | Mexico City | San Francisco
Shanghai | Tokyo | Toronto | Washington, D.C.

Bulk discounts available. For details visit:
www.amacombooks.org/go/specialsales
Or contact special sales:
Phone: 800-250-5308
Email: specialsls@amanet.org
View all the AMACOM titles at: www.amacombooks.org
American Management Association: www.amanet.org

This publication is designed to provide accurate and authoritative information in regard to the subject matter covered. It is sold with the understanding that the publisher is not engaged in rendering legal, accounting, or other professional service. If legal advice or other expert assistance is required, the services of a competent professional person should be sought.

The names of individual students referenced in this work are fictitious. Further, the student examples used herein do not represent any particular student or particular group(s) of students. Rather, these examples represent composite students, and cross-sections of various groups of students.

Library of Congress Cataloging-in-Publication Data

Deurlein, Rebecca.
  Teenagers 101 : what a top teacher wishes you knew about helping your kid succeed / Rebecca Deurlein, Ed.D.
     pages cm
  Includes bibliographical references and index.
  ISBN-13: 978-0-8144-3465-9 (pbk.)
  ISBN-10: 0-8144-3465-7 (pbk.)
  ISBN-13: 978-0-8144-3466-6 (ebook)
  1. Parent and teenager. 2. Teenagers. 3. Parenting. 4. Adolescent psychology. I. Title.
  HQ799.15.D48 3015
  305.235—dc23
                          2014020766

© 2015 Rebecca Deurlein
All rights reserved.
Printed in the United States of America.

This publication may not be reproduced, stored in a retrieval system, or transmitted in whole or in part, in any form or by any means, electronic, mechanical, photocopying, recording, or otherwise, without the prior written permission of AMACOM, a division of American Management Association, 1601 Broadway, New York, NY 10019.

    The scanning, uploading, or distribution of this book via the Internet or any other means without the express permission of the publisher is illegal and punishable by law. Please purchase only authorized electronic editions of this work and do not participate in or encourage piracy of copyrighted materials, electronically or otherwise. Your support of the author's rights is appreciated.

About AMA
American Management Association (www.amanet.org) is a world leader in talent development, advancing the skills of individuals to drive business success. Our mission is to support the goals of individuals and organizations through a complete range of products and services, including classroom and virtual seminars, webcasts, webinars, podcasts, conferences, corporate and government solutions, business books, and research. AMA's approach to improving performance combines experiential learning—learning through doing—with opportunities for ongoing professional growth at every step of one's career journey.

Printing number
10 9 8 7 6 5 4 3 2 1

To parents who just want to
understand and help their children . . .
in other words, to parents

CONTENTS

ACKNOWLEDGMENTS

I would like to thank the thousands of teenagers who have walked through my classroom doors over the years. In exchange for my instruction on sentence structure and classic literature, you taught me about the importance of laughter, perseverance, patience, and walking in another's shoes before issuing expectations and judgments.

I thank my family, the core of my existence and the foundation of my parenting insights. Jeff, my parenting partner and husband of twenty-six years, has been a model of acceptance and celebration of our children's individual personalities. Our children, Rachel and Jonathan, could not make me more proud and were a constant source of support and material for this book. I extend to them the utmost gratitude.

Thank you to all of the people who played a part in making this book happen, including my agent, Sheree Bykofsky; my editor, Ellen Kadin; and all of the behind-the-scenes people at AMACOM Books. Thank you to my friends who encouraged me to "tell the stories that need to be told" and to follow my dream to write this book. You are priceless.

Finally, thank you to my own parents, Grace and Jim, for setting the example of what great parenting should look like. I learned from the best, and I will forever treasure the lessons you taught.

INTRODUCTION

THERE IS A STORY I LIKE TO TELL MY STUDENTS ON THE first day of school that perfectly describes why I love teenagers. Yes, I said it. I love teenagers. I realize that this makes me a bit of an anomaly, and I'm okay with that. I sympathize with how hard they are to understand, and I get how difficult they can be to work with. I know all about their mood swings and unpredictable behaviors and inexplicable decision-making skills. But maybe after my story, you'll understand a little better why, despite all of that, I still have a profound appreciation for this misunderstood group.

Here's my story: When I walk into a roomful of people for the first time, introductions are made, and the most likely next question is, "So what do you do for a living?"

I smile and respond, "I'm a teacher."

Usually, the faces of the other people light up and they nod their heads appreciatively. "That's great!" a few say, grins spreading across their faces. "What grade?"

Now, I know what's coming next. It's become a game to me, timing how long it will take before the other people's demeanor changes to reflect the information I'm about to share.

"I teach high school kids," I say, and I start counting.

Within seconds, eyes widen, faces fall, smiles turn into frowns, and heads shake. The responses vary—"Oh my gosh, how do you do that?" "You're kidding? Why?" and in the South, "Oh, bless your heart"—but the sentiment remains constant: *Why in the world would anyone want to do that job?*

Remember, I tell this story to my students, and at this point, I have their rapt attention. *Where is she going with this*, they wonder? *It's the first day of school. Is she really going to tell us that everyone thinks we're monsters?*

I pause, and then I explain:

"The sad thing is that most people don't understand you. They don't get how awesome—and I mean that in the true sense of the word, as in 'filled with awe'—it is to be in the presence of your age group. When I try to put my finger on it, I picture a teenager, straddling an invisible line. On one side of the line is adulthood. I have heard teenagers like you share the most profound, insightful thoughts that just blow me out of the water. I've seen you empty your pockets so that strangers can have Christmas toys for their children. I've watched you stand in line to give blood and go out of your way to help someone whose locker contents have just spilled into the hallway. I've been flabbergasted by thoughts you've shared that are wiser than anything I've ever heard another adult say.

"But on the other side of that line is childhood, and you still have one foot firmly planted there. There isn't a day that goes by that you don't make me laugh over something silly or ridiculous that you do or say. You are full of life, invincible (if only in your own minds), and still childlike enough to be full of wonder. In short, you are incredibly unique, and I love spending time with you every single day."

I realize that this is an unusual take on our normal view of teenagers. Maybe it's how I've managed to teach for so long and how I continue to love my job while so many other teachers drop like flies. But it doesn't change the fact that you, and many, many other parents out there, try as you might, just don't understand teenagers.

You picked up this book because there is at least some aspect of your children that stumps you, keeps you up at night, or drives you batty. And you're not alone. The responses I've heard at countless functions over the years have proved to me that teenagers are an enigma to just about everyone, including themselves. Parents the world over are just like you—they want answers, not just to make their lives a little easier, but to help their kids grow into successful young adults. They want their home lives to be more peaceful, for daily activities to run more smoothly, and for their relationships with their teenagers to be closer, healthier, and more respectful. Believe me, you're in good company, and you've come to the right place.

What makes me an expert on teenagers? I've been a high school teacher for seventeen years, which means that thousands of teens with their own sets of challenges have passed through my door. I've supervised, sponsored, motivated, or counseled thousands more. While you have experienced only the teenagers in your own home, I've experienced all manner of kids who were reared by parents with a wide range of philosophies and beliefs. I've seen what kinds of kids have gone on to great success and what kinds have floundered for years because of, in large part, how they were parented. I've recognized patterns of behaviors, warning signs of self-destruction, and body language and words that imply problems and concerns. I've pretty much seen it all, and I will share with you what I have witnessed and how my experiences can help you as parents.

Regardless of your unique situation and family dynamic, it's likely that I've worked with children just like yours. I've taught in six schools, public and private, in four states; all grades; all socioeconomic backgrounds; all races and cultures; and all abilities, from special education to gifted and talented. My students, regardless of their situations, consistently earn the highest scores in the school on standardized tests in English, my subject area. This means that I find ways to motivate even those kids who seem unmotivatable. I have to. I'm a teacher. If I can do it with thirty kids in the classroom, you can do it with your own children, whom you know better than anyone. I'll share tips and strategies that will give you some insight into your kids so that you can motivate them at an entirely new level.

In my role as a teacher, I've always believed in developing relationships with parents and communicating with them clearly. Partnerships are crucial. I am with your children eight hours a day and see them in an environment where you will never see them. I watch them interact with their peers, handle or not handle stress, make decisions, work or not work, take advantage of or pass on opportunities, and even lie and cheat when they're afraid. I see how they act and speak when you're not there to watch them. I am your eyes and ears when you can't be there, and I have a lot to tell you about your kids. I will surprise you with their deeds—both good and bad—and help you to translate the information I share into better, more effective parenting practices.

I've also done my homework. I earned a doctorate in education after spending seven years in graduate school studying data on teenagers, researching best practices, and delving into the teenage mind. As a student and a researcher, I stepped outside of my own experiences and met with educational leaders around the nation to solicit and share ideas. I value the time I spent researching and working with other professionals to discover why kids do what they do, what they're thinking, and what others have discovered in their study of the teenage psyche.

Finally, I raised my own two teenagers, so I'm a parent just like you. My son and daughter were children with opposite-end-of-the spectrum personalities, learning styles, and interests. I was recently exactly where you are, and all of the angst and stress and worries are still fresh in my mind. But both of my children are making me proud as they make their way in the world. They are successfully pursuing their chosen fields and contributing to society, and they are happy and well-adjusted, with their priorities in place. That's what we all want for our children, and I want to help you work toward those goals right now.

As a mom, a veteran teacher, and a researcher, I will share what I have learned from my various roles. My teaching experience, knowledge, and personal dealings with my own children form the basis of this book. My advice, while based on sound principles and psychology, is real and timely and practical. Anyone anywhere can pull from the resources I provide to strengthen their relationships with their children and to parent more confidently.

And consider this, perhaps the most unique aspect of my relationship with teens: They *choose* to talk to me. I'm not their mom, or their therapist, or their friend. I am an adult figure whom they confide in, share their concerns with, and look to for objective advice. They talk to me about their parents and home lives, their dreams, and their frustrations. And without betraying their confidences, I will share with you the themes of those conversations and the insights I've gleaned over years of talking to and observing teens.

I am a unique resource with a fresh perspective on your kids. I offer information that you can't get anywhere else, and I will be straight with you. Some of what I say may hit a bit close to home, and some may not seem to apply to your situation at all. But while the chapters of this book cover a wide variety of topics, the parenting advice remains consistent throughout. Therefore, I encourage you to explore each chapter, even those that don't seem to apply, so you can see the importance of clear, consistent parenting.

By the end of this book, I hope you will have a new appreciation for teenagers and their remarkable ability to differentiate themselves from any other age group we encounter. I will help you to be right there with them, guiding them, teaching them, and helping them to keep their balance as that line they're straddling shifts and they begin to plant both feet in adulthood.

CHAPTER 1

How to Motivate Your Kids

FOR HUNDREDS OF YEARS, SCIENTISTS AND PSYCHOLO-gists have questioned and experimented with the motivations behind behaviors and responses. Clearly, it's not an exact science, or we would all be motivated all the time. We are reminded of just how far we have to go in this area when we look at teenagers. Branded as apathetic, teenagers often live down to that expectation, seemingly ambivalent about almost everything in their lives. How was your day? *Fine.* Did you learn anything in school today? *No.* Do you have any homework? *No.* Are you telling me the truth? *No.* One of the reasons we find the teenage years to be so frustrating is because our kids don't seem to care about much of anything. Or they care about things they shouldn't and don't care about what they should. Or they care about what *they* care about, not what *we* care about. And maybe that's the meat of it, the part that drives us absolutely crazy. Their priorities don't even begin to resemble ours, and we can't understand what they're thinking.

It's no wonder tensions run high when we live with teenagers. My experience has taught me that the typical home with teenagers looks something like this:

Mom and Dad get up early in the morning to prepare for their day. Teen stays in bed, despite the alarm going off at least three times. Mom and Dad fight with Teen over getting out of bed and making it to school on time. Teen gives every indication that he doesn't care. Mom and Dad both spend eight hours at work, often performing aspects of the job they dislike but do anyway. They return home to make dinner for the family, do dishes, pay some bills, and prepare for the next day, chores they don't want to do but they have to do to keep the home running. Sometime during the evening, they conduct a one-sided conversation with Teen that reveals absolutely no information about his day. They do not see him doing any homework, and when they ask him to pitch in with the household chores, he gripes and complains to the point that they'd rather just do it themselves than deal with his attitude. They talk to him one more time about joining a club or a sports team, but he says he doesn't want to and he's tired of hearing about it, so they drop it, hoping he will change his mind. They remind him that summer is coming and he will need to get a job, and he rolls his eyes, grabs the remote control, and tunes them out. Mom and Dad fall into bed exhausted, their own motivation zapped. Teen's motivation stays exactly where it was, reclining on the couch, mired in apathy.

If you can relate to the above picture, you know exactly what it's like to try to motivate an unmotivated teenager. To call it an exercise in frustration would be an understatement. We are working hard every day to provide a good life for our children. We know exactly what it's like to do what we have to do, even though we don't want to, because it's going to pay the bills, help us to reach our goals, be good for us in some way, or simply fend off undesirable outcomes. That's why it is particularly frustrating when we can't get our kids to see the value in hard work or to make sacrifices as a means to an end. It almost drives us to the point of desperation to just try to figure out what makes our kids tick.

Positive Reinforcement

Ivan Pavlov had no way of knowing that his experiment with dogs in the 1890s would yield such beneficial results for humans today. In an effort to study salivary glands, he noticed that dogs would begin to salivate involuntarily at the mere presence of food. Interestingly, when Pavlov rang a bell at the same time food was presented, dogs began to associate the bell with food. Even when food was not presented, dogs salivated when the bell was rung. Pavlov found that the reaction also worked in the reverse. If a stimulus became associated with a negative consequence, animals shut down or retreated completely because of stress or pain. Carl Jung stepped in to expand the experimentation to humans, finding that in much the same way, humans are motivated by positive stimuli and demotivated by negative stimuli.

This seems like a no-brainer, yet we forget all about these findings when we are dealing with teenagers. We forget that it is a basic desire of all humans to be acknowledged for positive behavior and contributions, and when we receive that acknowledgment, it increases the likelihood of more positive behavior on our part.

Let's apply this to a real-life situation. Imagine that your daughter, Ashley, never pitches in around the house. She watches her parents run up and down stairs, clean, carry laundry, and do yard work, and seemingly never feels the need to offer a hand. What are some possible reasons why Ashley doesn't participate in the household chores?

- She doesn't want to. Who in the world likes doing chores?
- She doesn't know she should. No one has ever expected it of her.
- She has done some chores in the past, and each time, someone has corrected her or gone behind her to "fix" whatever she did.

- She doesn't feel a sense of community or family. Instead, she has an "every woman for herself" mentality.

Think about it—her reason for not doing chores is very likely to fall into one of these four categories. It is unlikely that there is some deep-seated reason behind her lack of motivation; therefore, we shouldn't be afraid to tackle this problem head-on. If there are only four possible solutions, it won't be too difficult to turn this problem around.

Reason #1—She doesn't want to

This is the most obvious answer, and quite understandable. No one wants to do chores. The problem is that we need to in order to survive, thrive, and maintain our sanity. Ashley would need to if everyone didn't do it for her. She needs to eat, she needs to wear clothes, she needs to have a clear pathway to move from room to room. When she is on her own, either in college or in a job, she will need to handle all of these chores. Does she even know how? If she had to do her own laundry right this minute, could she? If she had to put together a healthy meal, would she know how to do it? The question of whether she wants to is really a moot point, because in a year or two or three, she will *need* to. Just as we encourage our children to set goals and work toward them, we should also be teaching them the steps along the way to become fully independent, and this includes doing unwelcome, tedious chores.

So let's address the tedium. It's real. It's unfortunate. And, like so much of our lives, it involves work we don't want to do but must. You know as well as I do that we all have to jump through hoops and do the unpleasant tasks in order to reach our goals. Heck, we need to do unpleasant and even miserable tasks just to get through any given day, right? We owe it to our children to teach them that lesson before it slaps them in the face in college and beyond. Let's be proactive by enlightening them early on that the road to success is paved with potholes, and they must navigate their way through and around them to get to where they want to be. In plain English, there are jobs we all do whether we want to or not. View them as a necessary evil, a means to an end. There is really no way around them, and the sooner your kids realize this, the better prepared they'll be.

So a simple response when Ashley states that she doesn't want to help with the yard work? "I hear ya. I don't want to do yard work either. But it needs to be done, and if we all help each other out, it won't take nearly as long. Then we can spend the rest of the day having fun. Let's go!" And then the work starts, because you can't relent when she argues or complains or says she's not going to do it. Take comfort in the fact that if you do this a few times, the hardest work will be over. You will have sent a clear message that opting out of chores is, in fact, not an option at all. You will have also taught your child that when you ask her do something, you expect her to do it. It will take only a few times, however, because you will also employ other methods of motivation that are much more pleasant (we will talk about these later), so that eventually, Ashley will see the value in the chores and assume a role in the family that involves cooperation and a fair division of the labor.

I don't feel like I can go on to the next option without emphatically restating this: Assume that your expectation will be granted and move on. When you frame your expectation as a request that you fear won't be fulfilled, trust me, it won't be. Teenagers are like bloodhounds when it comes to sniffing out hesitation. They will eat a teacher or an employer or a parent alive if that unfortunate person shows any kind of weakness. And they take a kind of pride in this. It makes them feel powerful in an otherwise powerless situation. Even if you don't feel it, you must display confidence, as if there isn't a doubt in your mind that your children will do what you just asked of them.

Reason #2—She doesn't know she's supposed to help with chores

I always like to give everyone the benefit of the doubt unless and until they prove they don't deserve it. In this case, I would assume that Ashley simply doesn't know or understand that she should be helping out. It's quite possible that Mom and Dad have assumed the role of housekeepers, and it has never even occurred to them to ask Ashley to help. Or it may be that they are afraid to ask for her help. After all, Ashley is really moody, and Mom and Dad are already walking around on eggshells in her presence. Why set her off by asking her to do something she'll never in a million years want to do? It's not a hill they're willing to die on, but it should be, because without an understanding of and appreciation for cooperation and responsibility, how far do you think Ashley will go in life, both personally and professionally? It's amazing what kids will do when a chore is presented not as a choice but an expectation. Mom and Dad simply need to let Ashley know that as a member of the family, she has responsibilities. Families pull together to keep a house in order and to share the load. And when they do, they establish buy-in. If they're the ones cleaning, they do everything in their power to keep the house clean. If they're doing laundry, they think twice before tossing a gently worn shirt into the wash. The ripple effect is far-reaching, and everyone is happier when the load is lightened.

Ashley isn't alone in living in her own world. Teenagers, especially, are notorious for it. The following is an actual conversation I had with one of my students, Will, about cleaning up after himself at lunch:

Me: Hey, you're not going to get up and leave that mess behind, are you?

Will (glancing at table innocently and shrugging shoulders): Ahhh, yeah. Who cares?

Me: Well, the next person who sits here.

Will: Oh, no worries, the janitor will clean it up. It's, like, her job, you know?

The next week, Will ended up in detention. In evidence that sometimes the wheels of fate are fortuitous, Will found himself on cafeteria duty. After he had served his time and returned to his normal routine, I noticed that he picked up his trash and threw it away without thinking twice.

Me: Hey, you cleaned up after yourself!

Will: Uhhhhh, yeah. These kids are pigs! I never want to have to clean up after them again.

Will didn't have a profound personality change in two weeks' time. He simply grew an awareness of others and the work involved in keeping a cafeteria clean, and this awakened a sense that he contributes to a world bigger than his own. Just as with Ashley, all it took was being on the other side.

Reason #3—Her efforts are not good enough

You would never say those words to Ashley, but are you inadvertently showing them through your actions? Say you ask Ashley to clean the family room, and your idea of clean is much different from hers. If you take the time to teach Ashley exactly what your definition of clean is, you have a right to be miffed if she does a halfway job. But many of us assume that the other person can read our minds and know exactly what our expectations are. We set our teens up for failure when we do this. It's unfair, and in this situation we have no right to be angry or frustrated when our child's output does not match our expectations. Besides, every person tackles a job differently, and as Momma always told me, there's more than one way to skin a cat. I have visited friends who have entirely different ways of running their households than I, yet their homes are managed efficiently, and their systems work for them. I am of a "less is more" decorating philosophy, but I've been in houses filled with knickknacks and memorabilia, and the home is a direct reflection of its inhabitants, as it should be. Just because your children are growing up in your house doesn't mean they have the same tastes and perspectives as you.

Imagine that you have delegated the cleaning of the family room to Ashley. You have explained what cleaning means: putting the clutter in its appropriate place; dusting the furniture, including removing and dusting whatever's on top; running the mop along the baseboards; and finishing with a thorough vacuuming. A half hour later, Ashley emerges from the family room mopping her brow and sighing loudly. You say, "Wait a minute. You've only been at this for a half hour, and it always takes me much longer." You walk into the room, run your finger along some random pieces of furniture, frown at the scattered magazines on the coffee table, and turn back to Ashley, who looks like she might consider running away at any moment. In an effort to be encouraging, you say, "Well, I guess this is okay. I don't think you could have possibly gotten it very clean in this amount of time, but it will do. Thank you," and applaud yourself silently for grinning and bearing it.

The problem is that when we want our teenagers to be stupid, they're not. They know when we've had an argument with a spouse, they know when we're trying to cover up anger or sadness, and they know when we disapprove, even when we think we're putting on a convincing show. With the above actions you just showed Ashley that (1) you don't trust her to do a good job and will follow after her to check, (2) her way of cleaning shows different priorities, and you don't approve, and (3) quick work automatically signals lack of effort or quality. And you thought you were doing well with your comments! And you were! Clearly, you could have done a lot worse, but instead, you thanked her for her contribution, which is crucial. But at the end of the day, the Big Question has to be asked: Next week, when it's time to clean the family room again, and every week after that, what is the likelihood that Ashley will do it, improve it, and feel a sense of accomplishment when she does?

B. F. Skinner was a behaviorist who sought to understand how consequences play a role in determining why humans act as they do. He created the concept of operant conditioning, in which behavior changes depending on the conditions following it. In his 1938 book, *The Behavior of Organisms: An Experimental Analysis,* Skinner identified three types of responses, or operants, that can follow behavior:[1]

1. **Neutral Operants.** These are responses that neither increase nor decrease the probability of a behavior being repeated. In Ashley's example, Mom would not say anything about the cleanliness of the family room but merely thank Ashley for doing her chore.
2. **Reinforcers.** These are responses that increase the likelihood of a repeated behavior. Reinforcers can be positive or negative. In this situation, assuming Mom wants Ashley to continue to clean the family room, she will tell her what a good job she did and how much she appreciates Ashley's newfound responsibility within the family. Ashley may not jump for joy when it's time to clean again, but she will now associate her efforts with positive reinforcement and good feelings. Please note that showing pleasure and encouragement about a job that doesn't really thrill you is not promoting unearned self-esteem or defeating your purpose. There is nothing wrong with adding a caveat: "One thing—next time you do

this, can you please just stack the magazines like this? I know it seems trivial, but it drives me nuts when they're all over the place." This is said with an "I know it's crazy, but it's just one of my things" tone that conveys it's a personal priority and one you would appreciate even though it doesn't matter to her. Consider it another feather in your cap that you just taught the lesson that you sometimes do things for other people even though you personally think it's stupid.

3. **Punishers.** These are responses that decrease the likelihood of a behavior being repeated. Punishment weakens behavior. Mom knew enough to not ground Ashley for doing a less-than-perfect job. If she hadn't been so wise and had actually punished Ashley for the work she did, she could have expected increased opposition and decreased work effort in the future. Any hope for cooperation would have gone down the drain, and Mom would have been in for a fight every week from that point on.

Knowing and understanding these operants is crucial. How you respond to your children's actions and what consequences they face as a result of their behavior will determine, almost entirely, their future behavior.

A TEACHER'S CONFESSION

Frequently, I am guilty of forgetting what I just told you, and am reminded after handing back student work. I watch faces fall and shoulders slump. I see kids show signs of complete dejection and hopelessness. Sometimes it is my fault for forgetting to note the positives or for mistakenly believing that the students will understand my hastily written feedback. Other times their responses have more to do with what kind of day they are having than anything I wrote on their papers.

They are human, just as we are. Some approach me and let me know that they don't like my feedback, while others complain to their friends. Their immediate reaction is less important, however, than the long-term ramifications. The true test of the impact of my words comes when the next paper is assigned. Will they listen and strive to improve, or will they slump farther into their seats and resign themselves to doing poorly? After seventeen years of collecting data on that question, I can say, unequivocally, that negative feedback rarely inspires a student to prove me wrong and do better next time. It isn't until I provide a sentence of encouragement or an acknowledgment of something they have done well that I see a spark in a kid who needs to improve. Every kid does something well. Our job is to notice when that happens and use it as a tool of encouragement that will prod children to work harder next time.

Reason #4—She doesn't have a sense of family as a community

Developmental psychologist Abraham Maslow created the now famous hierarchy of needs, a system that delineates various attributes that all humans need and desire in order to grow and mature. Later formed into a pyramid (see Figure 1), the hierarchy of needs begins on the most basic level of physiological needs, then moves upward until self-actualization is reached with maturity and growth.[2]

As you can see in the pyramid, once basic needs have been met, human beings are able to explore the next level. They will seek out love and belonging, and upon receiving it will develop self-esteem and confidence. Once this development has taken place, people can then mature intellectually and communally, with great awareness of moral and social issues. This is, of course, where we

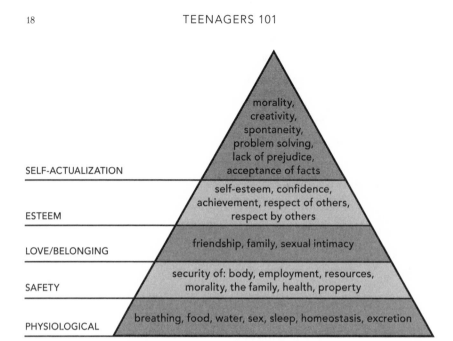

FIGURE 1: *Maslow's Hierarchy of Needs*

want our teens to go. We want them to enjoy success in their lives, but we also want them to be positive contributors to society.

So let's look at reason #4 for lack of participation on Ashley's part: She doesn't understand that she is part of a family and plays a crucial role in its development. Chances are that Ashley's physiological and safety needs are being met. She has the necessary foundation from which to build. She also receives plenty of love from her family; the question is whether she contributes to the "belonging" aspect of the model or is merely the recipient of those feelings. What does Ashley do to belong? What does she contribute? Do you see that if you have no expectations of Ashley to contribute to the household in some way, you are basically saying that she doesn't belong? Maslow clearly shows us that without a strong sense of belonging, Ashley will never progress to the higher stages we fully expect of functioning adults. She needs to feel needed and valued before she can develop the confidence to self-actualize. This happens in a few different ways, one of which we already discussed. You provide positive reinforcement when Ashley does something that you want her to do, something that is valuable and shows her investment in and commitment to the family. You accept that she will never do things exactly as you would, but you value her as an individual and appreciate what she brings to the family dynamic. As a result, she deepens her investment in the family because she wants to—she is internally motivated by feelings of belonging. It is a fundamental part of all teenagers that they crave and thrive on a feeling of belonging. If they don't belong in your family and are not receiving positive reinforcement from the role they play in it, they will seek to belong elsewhere. Why do you think gangs exist? Why do kids succumb to peer pressure and make poor decisions that they would never make individually? It's the desire to belong, and I'm sure you'd like that desire to be strongest within the family unit.

Psychologist Albert Bandura's concept of reinforcement stated that people are more likely to engage in certain behaviors when they believe they are capable of executing those behaviors successfully.[3] When they trust in themselves and experience positive reinforcement for their efforts, they eventually build self-efficacy, or self-understanding. This will be discussed at length in chapter 9, but let me state emphatically that there is a big difference between self-efficacy and self-esteem that arises solely from others telling you how great you are. We want our children to develop self-efficacy that is based on true, valid accomplishments, as this is what leads to genuine inner motivation.

Basically, Bandura's findings reveal that if we have complete faith that our children are capable of doing something and we convey that to them, they are likely to expend great effort in order to meet those expectations. When they enjoy some level of success as a result, this builds on their stores of self-efficacy, which then motivates them to try again, with greater success, and so on. Imagine it as a type of self-fulfilling prophecy. Obviously, you should expect some balking if this is the first time you verbalize expectations regarding a particular area, for instance, if your children have never done chores and now you expect them to. This is where modeling comes into play. You owe it to your children to first teach them how to do what is expected of them, then stand back and let them do it.

How do we apply this to Ashley? Chances are, Ashley has seen you clean the family room repeatedly over the years. You've modeled this behavior for her, but it's unlikely she's studied your routine and could repeat it exactly, nor should she. This is why you walk her through three to five basic expectations just before she begins. You are sharing with her your bottom line but trusting her to run with it. Then you set her free with complete confidence that she will do a fantastic job. You don't labor over your expectations, repeat them (unless she asks for clarification), nag her, or talk down to her in any way. Your attitude should reflect your belief that she is entirely capable of doing what you are asking her to do. It's an expectation, not a plea or a bargain or a strained hopefulness. When she sees your confidence in her abilities, she will try to live up to your expectations. Just so you know, she will also live down to them if you display little hope that she can do what you're asking of her. This is where we pull from all of the psychological and behavioral theories presented in this chapter. We model, we set high expectations, we encourage a sense of belonging, we provide positive reinforcement, and we clearly verbalize our needs. In the long run, not only will Ashley move up Maslow's hierarchy, but we may just become better parents—and better people—ourselves.

How can I be so sure of this? I have been in the position of taking over a class from another teacher midstream. We'll call that teacher Ms. Eeyore. Ms. Eeyore didn't look at her kids as blank slates with great potential; instead, she shook her head and lamented our futures under the "leadership" of this motley crew. I'm just going to say it: She thought her students were stupid, plain and simple. And to be honest, they pretty much lived down to that expectation. When I took over the class, I applied all of the principles I have discussed in this chapter. In a nutshell, I treated the kids like they were smart, and I expected them to act as if they were smart, and lo and behold, they did and they were. When someone told them they could do it, they did it. Sure, they reverted to their old ways plenty of times; they tried to be lazy and blame it on the fact that they had been told they were lazy, and so on. The change didn't happen overnight—no lasting change does. It was a process that included a pattern of positive responses, along with modeling and encouragement and clearly stated objectives. It was constructive criticism couched in recognition of strengths and improvements. It was kids doing what I knew they could because I believed, and then they did, in their abilities to learn.

Applying Motivational Techniques to Homework

I know what you're thinking: *This is all well and good, but what I really want to know is, How do I get my kids to do their homework without having to stand over them and threaten them?* This is an excellent question, but if you think about it, you've already been given the basic tools. You know now that positive reinforcement is the number one determinant of the probability that a behavior will be repeated. You know what your teens are seeking—a sense of belonging, a belief in their capabilities, parental acceptance and pride—and now you can use that knowledge to guide your words and actions in motivating your teens. If we put these theories and tools into practice, it might look something like this:

Imagine that you have never had a designated time or place for your son Mac to complete his homework. Over the years, you have learned from teachers that Mac's homework is completed sporadically, and the quality is inconsistent. You know you should be more involved, especially in knowing when homework is due, but you're also trying to step back and teach responsibility. After all, Mac will leave for college soon and needs to take charge of his own homework. But remember, that doesn't free you from parenting; it just changes *how* you parent. You know how important good study habits are to success. You know that distractions are detrimental to focusing on quality work. You know that Mac tends to procrastinate, and this often gets him into trouble. (We will cover getting organized in depth in chapter 11.) So you set up a modeling situation in which you not only tell Mac about the importance of getting his work done, you also show him.

Begin by choosing—with Mac—a designated workstation. It should be comfortable, but not so much so that he will drift off into slumber. It should be free of temptations, including social media, video games, and Mac's cell phone. Then Mac should decide on a homework time each day. Let's say he wants downtime when he first gets home from school and doesn't like to study on an empty stomach, so he chooses 7:00 p.m. as homework time. Your job is to make sure that he has eaten and sticks to the plan. Mac settles into his work station at 7:00 p.m., and after a few minutes, he seeks you out to let you know that he doesn't really have all that much work tonight, just a quiz to study for and that's it. This is where more modeling comes into play. You offer to quiz him on his words, showing him an effective way to test his knowledge of the content. Then you ask him what he can work on that will make his life easier tomorrow or further down the road. When is his next test? Can he study the content he's learned so far? Does he have any papers due, and can he begin work on those? Doesn't he need to finish that novel by next Friday, and why not take advantage of the time and read some now? You are teaching Mac how to be a good student, how to look beyond this moment and think in terms of goals.

His first, immediate goal is to study for tomorrow's quiz, so that takes precedence. However, he has other goals (tests, reading assignments, larger papers) that he is working on regularly. Many students (and adults!) struggle with motivating themselves to work on an assignment that is due several days or weeks from the present. In fact, according to Dr. Joseph Ferrari's 2010 research at DePaul University in Chicago, 20 percent of people identify themselves as chronic procrastinators.[4] This is a scary statistic because it means that one-fifth of our population is at risk of not meeting work deadlines, not paying bills on time, and not seeking medical treatment in time to stave off serious illness. This is something that could affect every area of Mac's life, and you want to help him overcome this weakness.

Here are some ways you can help Mac set realistic goals and work toward them in a timely manner:

- Mac should have his own calendar. It should be something he can freely access from anywhere, preferably his cell phone or electronic tablet. Everything Mac needs to do and every place Mac needs to be should be plugged into that calendar, with reminder alerts set to his liking. For instance, I set a reminder days in advance for schedule interrupters like doctor appointments. But I set only minute or hour reminders for tasks that must be completed or phone calls that need to be made whenever I can squeeze them in that day. Mac must decide how much notice he needs for each task.

- All of the substantial assignments on his schedule, such as lengthy papers, projects, and tests, should be "chunked" into smaller, more doable sections. For example, if he has a science project that includes research, an experiment, and an analysis of the findings, he should assign a personal deadline for each of these components. In his mind, the project has just become much more manageable, and he has ensured that he will devote enough attention and time to each part to truly learn from the project.

- Mac's work should be completed ahead of time if possible. Most students readily admit when they have waited until the night before to write a paper, but they don't need to: It is glaringly obvious in the number of typos, grammatical and mechanical mistakes, and lack of depth displayed in the content. If students commit to finishing a paper a day early, they will have the time to edit, proofread, and really think about what they have just said. Again, they will walk away from the paper having learned a great deal more than the students who hastily drafted it the night before.

- When Mac sits at his designated workstation at the agreed-upon time and completes his work, that dedication should be acknowledged in some way. And I'm not talking about methods of bribery that pay him to do what he should be doing already. I'm talking about giving him a hug, telling him that he did good work, or just merely treating him with respect and kindness. You can extend this affirmation to Maslow's belonging stage by doing a similar activity at the same time, for instance, reading the paper or a book, paying bills at the computer, working crossword puzzles—anything that models engaging the mind during a quiet time in the day. Now Mac is not alone while everyone else is out tossing the ball in the yard or going to a movie. Everyone is engaged in a similar activity, and Mac fits right in.

- Positive results should be acknowledged when they happen. Mac *will* see improvement if he employs these strategies. He will get much more out of his classes; he will become a more organized person; he will enjoy support, encouragement, and praise from his family; his own self-efficacy will rise; and he will develop life skills that will serve him academically and personally.

Methods That Should Be Used Sparingly, or Not at All

I am often asked how I feel about external motivators, such as paying for grades, offering a cell phone or new computer game in exchange for hard work, or treating kids to their favorite dessert for performing well in a dance recital. There is no doubt that external motivators work. A mouse can be trained fairly easily to step on a lever if cheese will drop down in front of him. A dog will perform a trick if it will earn her a bacon bone. A monkey will perform an impressive dance if he knows his favorite food is waiting for him. But I want you to notice three things: (1) these are animals, and we certainly don't think of our children that way, (2) all of these motivators serve short-term purposes, and (3) they all involve masters asserting their authority over lesser beings, with the lesser beings merely reacting and taking no part whatsoever in the thinking or decision making. They are puppets on a string, and that's all. I know that's not what you want for your children. You want them to act of their own accord and to make their own decisions. You don't want them to be controlled by others. Nor do you want them to become the kind of people who perform their duties only because they see the materialistic, immediate gain in doing so.

Now, not every external motivator will lead to selfishness and skewed priorities. Certainly it is wonderful to praise your

children's accomplishments, as we have discussed. And we can't
ignore the fact that a new cell phone is a powerful motivator. But
is there a way to have the best of both worlds—to offer extrinsic
and intrinsic motivators to reward in the present and build positive motivation for the future? I believe there is.

Let's imagine that Sylvia is making mostly Bs with a smat-
tering of Cs, and we are positive that all of those grades could be
bumped up one letter if Sylvia just tried a little harder. We've con-
firmed this at parent-teacher conferences, and we have checked
to make sure that Sylvia isn't overextended with too many activities or social functions. We know that Sylvia really wants an iPod
to use while running or working out at the gym. We know that it
could serve as a powerful motivator for her, and we'd like to cap-
italize on that without starting something that will require us to
spend a lot of money just to get our kid to do what she should be
doing already. So we have the following discussion to make our
intentions perfectly clear from the start:

Mom: We need to talk about your grades. You know that we have
always stressed living up to your abilities and doing your best work.
Your dad and I have talked to your teachers, and we're all in agreement that you're not exactly giving school your best effort.
Dad: As we've always said, your only job right now is to be a good
student, to get the most from your education. We'd like to see some
improvement in that area.
Sylvia: Yeah, but so much of it is boring and useless. When am I ever
going to use geometry anyway?
Mom: You might be surprised. I know you can't really see the big
picture yet, but even if you never use geometry again, you will have
gained something from the experience of learning it. There's always
a takeaway, even if the takeaway is that you'll hire someone else to
figure out the area of your family room and order your carpet, rather
than doing it yourself. (Humor is important—it lightens the mood!)

Dad: The point is that you have to learn it, whether you want to or not. You can be miserable while you're learning it, or you can decide to get as much out of it as you can. The same applies to every single area of your life. It's up to you whether you decide to be an unhappy person whom life happens to, or a proactive person who takes advantage of every opportunity. And by the way, which one of these people is most likely to be successful and happy?

Sylvia: (Says nothing, because that would involve admitting that Dad has a point, but the wheels are turning.)

Mom: Speaking of which, have you noticed that people who enjoy life and who can afford to buy the things that make them happy generally work very hard to create that life for themselves? If you want a great lifestyle, you have to earn it. You have to find ways to motivate yourself, even if it's just a means to an end.

Dad: So on that note, Mom and I have been talking. We feel that if you work hard, you're deserving of something that improves your lifestyle. Just as we work those extra hours so that we can afford to eat out once a week, you should also reap the benefits of extra work and effort. We know you've wanted an iPod for a while now . . .

Sylvia: Really? You're going to get me an iPod? You're the best!

Mom: Wait a minute. Before you get all excited, this is how this is going to work. First, you're going to demonstrate that you are taking your classes more seriously, that you are putting more time into studying, and that you are giving more effort to your work in general.

Sylvia: I can do that! I just didn't before because a B is good enough.

Dad: A B is good enough if that's all you can do. It's woefully inadequate if you're capable of getting an A. And it's not even the grades that we are focusing on here, although they do reflect what you know and can demonstrate. We are concentrating on how you are growing as a person, how you are preparing for your future, and what you are placing value on.

Mom: Dad and I will observe this on our own, but we will also speak to your teachers to confirm that they have seen an improvement in your work habits. When everyone is in agreement that you are living up to your potential, then we will reward that with an iPod.

Dad: But we want to make something perfectly clear—once we know what you are capable of, we will expect that effort to continue. And when it does, we will be proud of you, and you will be incredibly proud of yourself, and that's the best gift we could ever give you.

Sylvia: Does that mean that I can't earn any more great gifts that I really want?

Mom: We don't know yet. The rewards may vary, but they will always be there in one form or another.

Dad: So are you on board?

Sylvia: Are you kidding me? I can't wait to tell Becky!

Sylvia will face the challenges of school with a new motivation. She now understands that success and monetary rewards come as a result of hard work. She also has no guarantee that she will be monetarily rewarded for all of her future efforts, just as adults come to know and understand. But what will happen is that she will enjoy earning that iPod. She will build her self-efficacy and learn what she is capable of. And she will eventually do the work because of the good feelings it produces, the internal motivation. That will drive her further, and a mixture of external and internal motivators will fuel her passion to try and to succeed. What more could you want for your children?

Some Final Thoughts on Motivation

I'd like to leave you with some key ideas about motivation and its success, both inside and outside the classroom. Some are caveats, some are reminders, but all are crucial:

- Internal motivation is much more desirable than external motivation. Bribery can and does work, but it should be used minimally and as a jumping-off point. It should then be used sparingly and only when other motivators are hard to come by.

- Speaking of other motivators, let's not forget those that involve family time. Going out for ice cream, making a favorite meal, and letting your teens pick the movie to watch on Friday night are all viable incentives. External motivators don't have to be expensive; in fact, it's preferable if they're not.

- Pay attention to what excites your children. What are their passions and strengths? Use these to motivate as much as possible. If Nan loves computers and is a whiz at PowerPoint, encourage her to use it to complete a project. If Luke has always been a hands-on kind of kid and he is trying to decide on a science project idea, guide him toward an area that is more kinetic than cerebral. Know your kids and motivate them accordingly.

- Help your children set realistic goals and methods by which to reach those goals. Check in with them, but try to step back and trust them.

- Do not nag. Do not engage in a battle of the wills. No one ever wins in this situation. If you want to demotivate your children, nag them a little.

- Show your children the relevance of what they are being asked to do. There is always relevance of some sort. Help them to see that there is something to be gained from every situation.

- Make your children the integral part of any goal setting or plan developing. They must buy in to the plan from the start or it is dead in the water.

- Always point out the choices and options in any scenario. Once you've modeled this, step back and ask guiding questions so your children become adept at doing this themselves. They should always think about their options before they proceed. And they should know, unequivocally, that they have options and choices in every situation they encounter. Talk about a life skill that you want to foster now!

- Define what success looks like, and then celebrate when it is earned. A B may not ultimately become an A, but if your children learned the content and worked hard, the pride should still be there. In fact, maybe it should even be a little stronger, because you and your teenagers have successfully differentiated between a letter on a report card (which, sadly, may not truly indicate what your children have learned and often doesn't reflect effort) and true character and work ethic.

- Never, ever punish children with something you want to motivate them to do. Remember Ashley, of family-room-cleaning fame? What are the chances she would be motivated to clean if you use cleaning as a punishment for missing curfew? And Mac the procrastinator who doesn't like to do homework? What message would you send to him if you forced him to study, nose to the grindstone, an extra hour because he lied to you about where he was Friday night? If you want your children to appreciate the value of studying and be self-motivated to do it, don't present it as a punishment.

• Remember that people change because there is something in it for them to do so. Either they want to stop feeling a certain way or they want to start feeling another way. If you want to motivate your children, create consequences and rewards that are positive.

CHAPTER 2

How to Encourage Perseverance in the Age of Instant Gratification

I WANT YOU TO THINK BACK, FAR BACK INTO YOUR CHILD-hood. You were in the ninth grade and had to produce a research paper on cells. You had paid attention in class, but not well enough to earn a decent grade without doing some heavy reading on the side. So two weeks before the paper was due, you mapped out everything you would need to accomplish each night in order to finish the paper in time.

Your parents dusted off the "C" book in the family's *Encyclopedia Britannica* collection and you read. Then you reread, because the *Encyclopedia Britannica* wasn't exactly gripping. While trying to decipher the language of the text, you hand-wrote phrases and copied quotes on index cards. Five note cards later, you realized that you didn't have enough information and would need to take a trip to the library for more sources. Mom pulled the wood-paneled station wagon around, and off you went to spend hours in the quiet confines of the library.

Of course, you first had to work your way through the card catalog, followed by locating the books on a dusty shelf and perusing them all, only to discover that they were written at different levels and sometimes even contained conflicting information. You checked out what you could and took notes from what you couldn't. The days that followed were filled with more note taking, creating an outline, writing a rough draft, having Mom and Dad mark up said draft, rewriting, and then finally sitting down at the typewriter to complete the paper, all the while praying that you wouldn't make a mistake and have to pull out the correction tape. Once the body of the paper was completed, you added your footnotes, paying careful attention to the formatting guidelines the teacher had requested. You double-checked your margins and page numbers, and, with the final product stapled, you breathed a sigh of relief as you handed it in, thinking that you knew more about cells than you ever wanted to.

Unless you later went on to become a writer or an English teacher, chances are that your memories of those papers are not positive. They were time consuming and difficult. The books on cells were boring and too academic to enjoy. The whole process was so labor intensive as to be a turnoff, something you would not want to repeat, even as an adult. Yet for all of your complaints, you now see the value in that endeavor. Yes, it gave you a much better understanding of cells, but it goes much deeper than that. Think about the skills you acquired by working through this process. You learned:

- How to form a plan and the steps required to reach your goal
- How to research, choosing beneficial sources over those of little use
- How to glean meaning from more formal, scholarly language and transcribe that into your own words
- How to organize each day in order to meet a deadline
- How to persevere by doggedly reading through sources,

writing and rewriting, accepting constructive criticism from Mom and Dad, and surviving typing

- How to produce something in the requested format, even if you thought that format was ridiculously rigid
- How to synthesize various pieces of information to draw your own conclusions
- How to produce a quality product that met the expected standards

If you look over this list, you see not just a series of skills for a science class but actual life skills. All of that hard work benefited you in ways you never even considered. Each time you worked through a difficult process, you gained or strengthened the characteristics that have made you who you are today. That's why the older generation tends to value honest work and tenacity—you know that it has made you better people.

That brings us to today's teenagers. It's now 2014, and Jose comes home with a research paper assignment on cells. The paper is due in two weeks, but he knows it won't take that long to write. He also knows, however, that his procrastination has gotten him into some serious sweatfests in the past, so he allows himself one week to write the paper. Proud of his plan, he puts the paper out of his mind and concentrates on his regular homework, baseball practice, Facebook, and his favorite TV show. A week passes and it's time to get started.

With Facebook still open on one screen and his cell phone by his side, Jose types "cells" into Google and within seconds has access to hundreds of articles. He starts at the top and clicks on the first entry. When the article pops up, he scans the first couple of sentences to determine if he can understand or is willing to read the article. In one minute, he dismisses the first and clicks on the second. When the second proves to be useful, he hits "Print," clicks out of that site, and moves on to the next. Within a half hour, he has found five sources and printed out the content. He has also responded to some texts and updated his Facebook status to "Ugh! I hate this science paper!"

The next night, Jose pulls out a highlighter and quickly scans the reading, highlighting important ideas or quotes he can add to his paper. There is no need to handwrite anything or to create source cards, as every piece of information he needs is right there on the printout. Finished for the night, he sets the highlighted articles aside until the next evening, when he sits down at his computer. Referring to the articles, he copies the information and changes a few words. His computer is already set to the proper format, his misspellings are automatically corrected as he types, and grammar check lets him know when he has a fragment or a run-on sentence. He uses his online thesaurus to pump up his vocabulary and tweets, "Who cares about cells anyway? #sciencesucks."

Next, Jose rereads what he wrote and copies and pastes the text to reorganize it. He then plugs his source information into easybib.com, which seamlessly formats the information. His final product is just short of the page requirement, so he makes the font one size bigger, increases the margins just enough so the teacher won't notice, and voila! The paper now meets all of the teacher's requirements. He hopes that he changed his sources' words around enough, and he prays that his teacher will overlook the fact that one of his sources was a blog written by a teenager. He's just glad that he didn't wait until the last minute like his friends did.

Throughout this entire process, Jose has taken phone calls from friends, followed the latest saga unfolding on Facebook, and sent and received hundreds of texts. At any given time, he was performing three or four tasks, not to mention fielding interruptions from family and life in general. Was his way of writing the paper better or worse than yours? Did he accomplish the same final goal that you did? Did he acquire the same skills? Here is what he likely took away from the experience:

- How to use the most valuable resource at his disposal—the Internet—to find the information he needs
- How to read critically to find the main idea
- How to use technology to quickly produce a paper that meets formatting requirements and is mostly grammatically sound
- How to perform multiple tasks and think on different levels simultaneously
- How to begin to discern between reliable and unreliable sources (he didn't actually get there, but at least he realized there was a difference)
- How to plan ahead and meet a deadline

As you can see, the life skills obtained are similar, and he managed to meet the deadline in half the time. Today's teens certainly have turned expediency into an art form. If you've ever watched your children text, type, or multitask, it is truly stunning to note the speed with which they work. Technology can be a beautiful thing, and the ease with which Jose completed this assignment is a testament to that.

However, note which life skill is missing from the above list: perseverance, identified here as working through numerous steps—some that seem on the surface to be unnecessary or at least contrary to what one wants to do—to meet a long-term goal that is weeks away.

Here we see the double-edged sword that is technology. It makes everything more efficient, but there is danger in that efficiency. When you plodded through encyclopedias and library books, you knew that those sources were reliable. The authors had been vetted, the books had passed through a rigorous publishing process, and the information had been validated. The Internet, however, is an open forum. Anyone can post an article or set up a web page and share knowledge, thoughts, or opinions with the world. While this yields a bountiful harvest of ideas, it doesn't distinguish between founded and unfounded ones. It is up to the researcher to take the time to check an author's background, and children today rarely do that. They want their information fast and easy, and this makes them highly susceptible to baseless opinions.

As a teacher, I see that this drive for quick information permeates teenagers' lives. Smartphones have eliminated the need to do any kind of legwork to find an answer to a question. Kids don't even need to type in their requests anymore; they can simply use voice-recognition technology and speak their request! As parents, you know exactly what I'm talking about. You are aware of how technology has affected your children's social lives, both for the better and the worse. You know how much they rely on their cell phones, and if you can afford to provide them with computers or tablets, you know how much time they spend on those devices, too.

There's no denying that technology has provided us with abundant opportunities for learning. Teachers have seen increased interest in every subject area thanks to interactive whiteboards, YouTube video tutorials, tablets, laptops, and even the ubiquitous cell phones. But as is the case with much of technology, it's an advancement that sometimes does the opposite, moving us several steps back in other areas of intellect or socialization.

The Curse of Technology

Let me tell you what you don't see: how technology and its ensuing instant gratification have negatively affected children in the classroom. This can best be illustrated through a typical fifty-minute class experience with twenty-five seventeen-year-olds studying *Macbeth*.

The students weren't exactly thrilled to hear that we would begin with a study of Shakespeare.

"Seriously, why are we reading something that was written in the 1600s?" Hayley asked. "That stuff is so old, and I heard that no one can even understand the way it's written. What's the point?"

I have this conversation every year, so I was prepared. "Just wait until you see how and why he wrote the way he did. When I get through explaining everything that made him so unique, trust me, you'll be impressed."

Darius's hand shot into the air, "Hayley's right. I even tried reading a couple lines from my brother's book when he was reading it, and it made no sense at all."

"Well," I replied patiently, "that's what I'm here for. I'll teach you how to read it so that it makes sense, and before you know it, reading Shakespeare will be almost as easy as reading anything else."

"Who reads?" quipped Larry. "When I have to read stuff for school, I get those books on tape and listen to them in the car. It's sooo much easier."

"Where do you get those?" asked Julie. "I'd so much rather listen to it than try to read it myself."

Just then, my student without a filter (there's at least one in every class) piped up, "You guys are doing way too much work. Just read the SparkNotes! I never read a single book for English class last year, and I still passed the class just from reading SparkNotes."

At this point, I stepped in to facilitate the conversation. I discussed the good and bad inherent in audiobooks and how much we cheat ourselves when we read summaries of books rather than the books themselves. Plowing ahead, I began my discussion by posing the question, "Does anyone know if Shakespeare was married?"

Out came the cell phones. Sarah was the first to speak, literally fifteen seconds after I asked the question. "Oh my God, Shakespeare was *gay?* Get out of here!"

"Wait, what are you talking about? Is that true?" A flurry of questions accompanied twenty-five Google searches as students attempted to find the same information. It didn't take long for them to find articles about Shakespeare's married life, his alleged infidelities, and yes, even suppositions that he was gay. I seized the opportunity to discuss the various sources we can find on the Internet and how we can determine if they are reliable. It was an unplanned learning experience, but we needed to get back to the topic at hand. I encouraged the students to use their technology responsibly to enhance the lesson, and by the end of the fifty minutes, the students had an appreciation for why we study Shakespeare.

But this was just the beginning. The next day, when we began to read the play, you can imagine how many lines we got through before the following conversation took place:

"What is this? I can't even read this. Is this supposed to make sense?"

"Just take your time and try to think about what the character is saying as you're reading the lines aloud," I advised. "If you think about the meaning and not the words, you won't notice the words so much and it will all start to make sense. Take your time."

But taking their time is not a teenage strength. They took turns reading, stumbling over the words, quickly getting exasperated, and generally complaining that it was just too hard to understand. And this was after one page.

Over time and with much prodding, most of the kids did hang in there and eventually realize that Shakespeare's bark is much worse than his bite. When they gave themselves the chance, they managed to understand his language and lessen their fear of overcoming a new challenge. And some, I'm sadly confident, read the SparkNotes instead. But regardless of the end result, they all began by trusting what they had heard from others, what they found on the Internet, or what they quickly surmised by merely looking at the words in front of them, rather than endeavoring to discover answers for themselves.

Sarah from this scenario is a typical teenager. She jumped to an immediate conclusion based on the very first source that popped up in her web search. With no time to think through her findings or consult other sources, she blurted out an insinuation, thereby passing on possibly erroneous information to her classmates. For their part, the other children wasted no time jumping on the bandwagon to validate the information. In addition, many kids brought negative preconceived notions to the task based on nothing but what they had heard from their peers. It didn't occur to them that if they gave the play a chance, they might have an entirely different opinion. And they definitely never concerned themselves with the possibility that their negativity might rub off on others. It was a classic case of speaking before thinking, and it's a huge problem with today's teenagers.

In their defense, it's not all their fault. They have several factors working against them, and one of them is biological. Impulse control is located in the lateral prefrontal cortex of the brain. This part develops slowly over time, often not reaching full maturity until well into adulthood. Teens simply don't have the control that older adults have, so we have to be patient when it comes to dealing with their outbursts and quick conclusions. It helps to know about this biological aspect because this part, at least, is out of our children's control. And believe me, they know they're impulsive and they don't like that about themselves. They often regret their words and actions and question why they can't control themselves better. This aspect of being a teenager is quite difficult for them. If you've ever said something without thinking, recognized it, and immediately regretted it, you know exactly how a teenager feels on a regular basis.

As you saw in the cell-essay scenario, another major factor contributing to children's impulsivity and subsequent need for instant gratification is their ability to get instant answers to any questions they have. The minute a question pops into their minds, they find the answer using an electronic device. We adults probably use and appreciate this ability, too. But remember when we had to actually think it through and stretch our memories? There was a time when we regularly counted money at the store, figured out percentages in our heads, calculated the square footage of a room, or simply added and subtracted using nothing but our brains. But now, kids don't have to think about these things. They whip out their cell-phone calculators and let their fingertips do the thinking. Now, I would never begrudge them this convenient and helpful tool. Heck, I do the exact same thing now that I can, so how could I blame them? But make no mistake, it *is* making a difference in their ability to problem solve on their own. It *is* keeping them from thinking and exploring creative options to reach a conclusion.

I had a favorite assignment that I gave my students when we finished reading a novel. In an effort to change with the times and engage the kids at their level, I came up with the idea of incorporating music into a novel study. The students could choose to demonstrate their understanding of *Catcher in the Rye,* for instance, by creating a CD that reflected the main character, Holden Caulfield. The CD had to contain ten songs they would give Holden, along with an explanation for their selections using sound argument based on their reading of the text. I loved this assignment because it allowed students to be creative and gave them choice, plus it encouraged them to express their individuality. An added bonus was that it wasn't a paper that could be found online, and SparkNotes wouldn't help at all. I saw it as a win-win for me and my students.

In the first couple of years with this assignment, the projects were astoundingly good. The students thoroughly enjoyed the critical thinking aspect of the work and the fact that they could interpret Holden however they liked just as long as they could back it up with textual evidence. They took great pride in presenting their compilations and enjoyed each other's ingenuity. They learned from one another and really, really thought about the text.

A few years later, I noticed that several students, even those who had no association with each other, had chosen the same songs for their playlist. What was happening? On a whim, I went to the Internet and did a search for "Catcher in the Rye songs." And lo and behold, various song suggestions popped up, and they were the exact songs "selected" by the students over and over again. Here I was patting myself on the back for coming up with an intellectually challenging but absolutely enjoyable assessment for my students, and here they were Googling it. All of the learning, the critical thinking, the creativity, and the individualism had been usurped in an effort to avoid the process and skip right to the result.

This is what I mean when I say that for all of the benefits of technological development, it also comes with a curse. A lack of patience pervades this generation because it has to wait for very little. Instant information, clicks of buttons to change channels, iPods that go directly to their favorite music, multitasking at every bend—it's enough to make you wonder what you can possibly do to reap the benefits of these advancements while minimizing the negative impacts on your children.

Thinking Through Options

One way to begin is by making thinking through problems part of their everyday routine. This is difficult to do because generally, we know the answers or solutions to most of our kids' problems. It is much easier to provide those answers than it is to watch children struggle through them. But remember the research paper you did in the ninth grade and the life skills you acquired by working through that process. These skills can come from various avenues. If you're an athlete, think about the level of commitment you reached, the pain you endured, the sweat equity you invested to overcome obstacles and reach your goals. If you have a physical disability, ask yourself how struggling with the challenges of that disability has strengthened your resolve and brought out attributes you might never have discovered had it not been for those challenges. If you are a single parent, you may have found your strength only after facing a host of difficulties and putting in the work of two people. Regardless of your circumstances, you know that facing down whatever life has thrown at you has made you a stronger person. It is the same with your children, and you must be careful not to deprive them of the opportunity to think through problems and pursue solutions rather than having the answers provided.

Let's begin by getting kids to patiently think through options before making decisions or jumping to conclusions. Remember, their impulsivity is biologically inherent, but you can create situations that encourage time and reflection.

In open-ended discussions with your teenagers, try the following:

- Wait for an answer. Get comfortable with silence. Studies show that increasing wait time for an answer (we're talking seconds, not uncomfortable minutes) elicits a greater number and variety of answers, makes not answering a nonoption, and encourages discourse among the people in the room—more back and forth rather than the dominance of one person's opinions or ideas.

- Do not be so quick to validate or confirm an answer. This squelches further thought and discounts other alternatives before they are even formed.

- Avoid posing questions like, "Do you understand what this decision will lead to?" or "Haven't you ever experienced this before?" If your children answer honestly, they may risk looking like fools, and no one wants to look foolish.

- Don't suggest the answer in the question. Have you ever taken a survey that was clearly designed to elicit desired responses? We tend to do the same thing when we talk to our children. We suggest the answer we want by formulating the question with a strong bias. For instance, "Would you say that piano is your most worthwhile activity?" would be better framed as "What activity do you think has been most worthwhile for you?" With the first question, your children won't really think through the matter because the answer is already supplied to them. Very little actual thinking will take place. The framing of the second question, however, requires thoughtful reflection.

- Assume that your children are intelligent enough to work through complex problems with the proper guidance from you. If you don't believe they are, they won't believe it either. They will become dependent on you for all of their decisions when they should be trusting themselves to make greater decisions as they mature.

Once children become comfortable with taking their time and processing problems, they will learn that the best answers are not necessarily the first ones. They will be less likely to believe the first answer or explanation they encounter. Warning: This may make your job as a parent a little tougher. They may begin to question you and become more aware of their ability to argue a point with you. This can be exhausting, but if you keep your eye on the long-term reward—children who think independently and have minds of their own—you can practice patience and strengthen your own critical thinking skills as well.

Applying Critical Thinking

The next step in this process is applying critical thinking to a task and hanging in there until the task is complete. I don't think anyone would argue that perseverance, tenacity, and work ethic aren't absolutely crucial to success and happiness in life.

Again, your own perseverance will be tested, but following the practices below will pay great dividends in the end:

- Involve your kids in at least one sport and encourage them to carry what they learn on the field through other areas of their lives. It's not enough to just make an appearance at a practice or game. Practice should include working on skills at home, attending every week regardless of whether children are in the mood, playing positions as decided by the coach, participating in drills that may not make sense to children, and generally committing fully to the requirements of team participation.

- Locate outside activities in which your children must show responsibility and pledge a certain amount of time to a task. This may include an after-school or weekend job, involvement in the arts, community service, leadership in a school or church organization—anything that places them in a long-term situation with regular participation. Children who try out for a role in a play, learn lines, rehearse, and perform gain an understanding that there is an important process to be followed before they will meet success. The more opportunities they have to experience the benefits of hard work the more they will treasure the value.

- Don't let them quit unless and until they have honored their commitments. Most adults admit they wish they had continued with their violin lessons or tried out for the varsity football team in high school. Laziness, boredom, fear, and insecurity can all play parts in children's desire to drop out of activities. I have met very few teenagers who hate their parents for making them continue with an activity. Even in the midst of it, they see the value and understand why their parents are pushing them. I trust that they will appreciate it even more when they are adults. Conversely, teenagers regularly confide to me that they regret dropping out of activities and wish their parents had pushed them to stay in. I would never suggest that a child who is miserable or suffering from anxiety be forced to continue a hated activity. But I think there is a huge lesson to be learned that when you start something, you finish it. If at all possible, children should finish out the school year or season and then revisit their participation for the future. And remember, coaches, music teachers, club sponsors, and even bosses are your allies. Talk to them to determine what you can do to help your children enjoy and benefit from the experience. Sometimes a minor tweak in the process can make all the difference.

- Let them deal with the consequences when they don't put the effort in. Some kids will only learn from trial and error. These are usually the ones who haven't developed their critical-thinking skills or learned to think through the consequences of their actions. These kids often won't learn until they are affected negatively by their actions. But they will learn if given the chance to face the consequences of their decisions. If they didn't study, it's probably fair that they don't pass the test. If they didn't read the book, they should not come out of the class discussion with a passing grade. If they plagiarized content from a source because they didn't want to take the time to write their own words, then they likely deserve the zero on that paper. Let them take it. The next time they will think twice, and that means they are beginning to think critically.

It won't take your kids long to realize that the sweetest successes come from the hardest work. They will begin to enjoy that true sense of accomplishment that creates greater motivation to accomplish more. Eventually, they will go off to college and the real world with work ethic and drive. And they will learn to appreciate the journey.

CHAPTER 3

Too Old to Run to Mom or Dad: When to Get Involved and When to Step Back

O NE OF THE MOST CHALLENGING ASPECTS OF BEING a parent is knowing when to get involved and when to step back. We have been the number one advocates in our children's lives since their birth, and letting them take the fall runs completely contrary to everything our hearts and minds tell us to do. How do we go from being in control of every aspect of their day to releasing them to high school for eight hours and trusting that they will take ownership of their education? The fact of the matter is that it is a weaning process. Just as we weaned our babies off the bottle or breast, we must wean our teenagers from dependency of other kinds as well. This doesn't happen overnight. After all, if we've been handling things for fourteen years, we can't very well step back, wipe our hands of our children, and let them head toward the cliff. The weaning process must be just that—a process, but done thoughtfully and with conviction, it can be pleasant rather than painful, encouraging rather than frustrating.

When it comes to your teen's education, one thing is perfectly clear: Teachers want your involvement and support. They want it badly enough that they named parental involvement the single most important factor in student success, according to a 2012 study by Scholastic and the Bill & Melinda Gates Foundation.[1] So don't misunderstand—your involvement is desired because teachers recognize the value of a partnership with parents. Note the word *partnership*. It suggests that teachers and parents should work together with a shared interest in the student's success. Trust me, students will give every indication that they don't want their parents and teachers talking. They know that if a partnership is formed between parent and teacher, they will no longer be able to divide and conquer. Some will understand and appreciate that the partnership means the adults in their lives care, but many won't see it that way. It doesn't matter. When it comes to children, we can't always make decisions based on what they like; we have to make decisions based on what is best for them.

Two Very Different Stories

A partnership works two ways and ultimately benefits students to a great degree, while modeling cooperation and respect. I had a student, Grace, who was an extremely talented dancer and who performed in numerous productions outside of school. This had required her to be homeschooled for most of her life, but her parents felt it was important for her to have a few years of public education, so she was newly enrolled at my school. I knew all of this because her parents sent me an email introducing themselves and explaining Grace's background. Naturally, they were concerned about the transition and huge changes that would take place, and they thought it important that I have this information. I appreciated it and told them so in a brief reply. I offered to keep an eye on Grace and alert them to any concerns.

As it turned out, Grace was a mature, responsible young woman who self-advocated and managed all of her responsibilities with aplomb. But that extra bit of knowledge I had received from her parents reminded me to make sure she had a partner during group work, to subtly observe her interactions with other students, and to help ensure that she assimilated into the public school peer environment. When her parents showed up for open house, we were able to assure each other that Grace appeared to be fine both at school and at home, and it was obvious that we both appreciated the role one another played in this success. So partnerships don't need to be time consuming; they just need to be established from the onset and valued on both ends.

Partnerships are especially valuable when a problem arises. Scott was notorious for being unprepared for my class. I have a policy that I always address every issue with students first, out of respect for them and the partnership we share. Sometimes I will address the same problem several times before I feel the need to contact a parent. In this case, I had tried working with Scott with little success, so I reached out to his mom via email. I shared my concerns and asked for her support at home. I warned her that Scott's grades were dropping and that the most important area on which he needed to work was getting his assignments in on time. She immediately replied and said she would talk to Scott about the issues, and I was hopeful that her involvement would help to engage Scott a little more.

Unfortunately, it didn't happen. The next time Scott came to class without his work, he received a zero for the assignment. As soon as Scott went home that day, he complained to his mother about the zero, and she quickly drafted an email asking me to reconsider the grade. She explained that Scott was just a teenager and still learning about responsibility, and he should be given another chance to prove himself. I had talked to Scott about his work several times, shared my concerns with his mom, and thought that I had gained a partner who would impress upon Scott the importance of due dates and deadlines. However, Scott and his mother had their own agenda. The teacher-parent-student partnership dissolved when the grade was disappointing. In this way, the grade trumped the learning. Scott suffered in many ways from this splintered partnership. He never learned to take responsibility for his own work, but he did learn that he could play one adult against another to his advantage.

Now, the question is, where do you fall on the spectrum between Grace's and Scott's parents?

Ask yourself if you've ever said any of the following to your child:

- "Your teacher doesn't know what she's talking about."
- "You got a C on that paper? Don't worry; I'll take care of this."
- "Your teacher said what? You better believe I'm following up with the principal on this."
- "I don't understand what you're supposed to do with this project. I'll email the teacher."
- "Do you ever pay attention in class? What is wrong with you? Do I have to come to class with you to get you to pay attention?"
- "Let me see that assignment; I'm sure I can figure it out."
- "Don't turn in that paper until I've had a chance to edit it. I've seen your writing, and you need all the help you can get."

If you've used any version of any of these statements, even with good intentions, chances are good that you do not think of yourself as a teacher's partner or as a parent who trusts your children's abilities to problem solve. You want to intercede on your children's behalf, but in doing so, you are sending the message that the teacher is in the business of customer service and the students are incapable of getting the proper service on their own. You are operating under the assumption that with pressure and scare tactics, you can manipulate your children's opportunities and grades. But what's even more worrisome is that you are also letting your teens know that they are incapable of handling their own problems and need you to step in and "fix things." You are relegating them to the position of passive observers rather than active learners. Education is now something that happens to them, or for them, rather than something they control. And you are slipping down that dangerous slope into helicopter parenting, something that will hurt both you and your children in more ways than one.

Helicopter Parents and the Tethered Generation

The term *helicopter parent* was coined by Foster W. Cline and Jim Fay in their 1990 book *Parenting with Love and Logic: Teaching Children Responsibility*.[2] They used it to describe parents who hover over their children, overseeing all aspects of their lives, especially schooling. It is quite telling that the term has become part of our everyday vernacular, as overprotective parents are becoming more the norm than the exception. The term has paved the way for variations on the theme, including the increasingly popular *lawnmower parents*, those who try to remove all the obstacles and create a smooth path for their children.

Add to this social issue the fact that kids can now be reached via cell phone wherever they are, day or night, and the situation becomes even more precarious. The term *tethered generation* describes a group of kids who are in constant communication with their parents. Gone are the days when kids went out and parents simply waited up for them to make sure they got home safely. Today we can check on them ten times in one night if we want to. This may sound like an improvement in regard to child-parent communication, and in many ways it is, but how much potential abuse does this advancement bring? Not only can we reach our kids to ensure their safety, but they can reach us to ask us any question they have, solve any problem that arises, or ride to the rescue when the going gets tough. Neither children nor parents are completely free to explore their lives outside of these restrictive roles because with one ring of the telephone, they are reminded of them.

CASE IN POINT

"How do I unfreeze the locks of the car so I can get to work?" my twenty-one-year-old daughter asked one morning via cell phone. Even though I had lived most of my life in the South and had limited experience with Chicago winters, I thought about it, gave her some suggestions, and solved the problem for her. She gratefully accepted the advice and hurried to work, none the worse for wear. But what would have happened if she hadn't been able to instantaneously call me the second the problem occurred? What if she had had to think about it? Come up with solutions? Experiment to see which option worked? What if she had had to work it out, without the benefit of Mom's or Dad's experience or wisdom? She may have been a little late to work, but I'm fairly confident she would have come up with the same ideas I did, tried them, found success, and always known from that point on that she is capable of solving problems on her own.

The problem with the tethered generation is that there is little room to breathe, on either end. Your kids leave for high school in the morning, and for the next eight hours, they should be independent of you. Instead, they use their cell phones (usually in bathroom stalls so they don't get caught) to tell you they bombed the test they thought they did so well on. You reply, "We'll see about that!" and the cycle begins (see Figure 2).

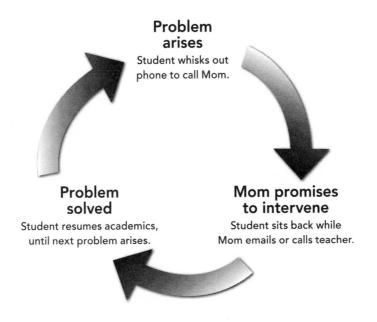

Problem arises
Student whisks out phone to call Mom.

Mom promises to intervene
Student sits back while Mom emails or calls teacher.

Problem solved
Student resumes academics, until next problem arises.

FIGURE 2: *The Problem/Solution Cycle*

And just as children rely on the phone to call parents, parents rely on it to stay in constant contact with children, even when the children are eighteen and legal adults. Remember the days when we were in college and our parents were lucky to reach us once a week on the one public phone in the dorm hallway? Now parents call their college-age kids multiple times in one day just to chat. In this way, eighteen-year-olds never have to solve any problems on their own because they know that Mom or Dad is likely to call before the day is out, ready and eager to offer advice and counsel.

So how do we find a happy medium between offering the support and encouragement that teachers, coaches, and employers desire and tying our children to us as if they were still on the umbilical cord? Let's go back to the concept of weaning. Animals instinctively know they must encourage their offspring along. Birds eventually push their young out of the nest. Mammals know when the time comes to nudge their young away from the teat and toward a diet more appropriate for their growing young. As parents, we thrill at the small steps our children take. We see it as the natural progression of things and encourage our children's first steps, potty training, and introduction to kindergarten. But something happens when our kids get to high school. Perhaps it's the realization that these are our last years with them. Perhaps it's the fear that they are old enough now to make really stupid decisions that could affect the rest of their lives. Perhaps it's their natural pulling away from us and our desire to hold them close just a little bit longer. Regardless, the result is too much parent involvement in areas where kids should be permitted to learn from their own mistakes.

Ironically, this desire to overprotect our children is actually hurting them in more ways than one. When we are rearing children who can't even attend college without parental intervention, that's a problem. Professors report that for the first time in generations, parents are demanding explanations for grades, attempting to attend conferences, and involving themselves in scheduling and course selection. The intervention subsequently brands students as children, and the regard professors had for those students quickly diminishes. High school teachers often feel the same way when parents intercede in everyday situations that should be handled by students. In Scott's case, I would have had much more respect for him if he had approached me about the zero, expressed regret, and offered a solution. Instead, he expected his mother to do the hard work that he was unwilling to do. If you, too, have acquiesced to your teens' requests to do the same, you have undermined their ability to problem solve, communicate with superiors, and advocate for themselves. These are life skills—some argue the most important and crucial life skills of all—and if your children don't learn them now, they will learn them later, with greater and more dire consequences.

Let Them Practice

If your goal is to raise children who can tackle problems as they arise, then you must let them practice doing so. If you want your children to be able to articulate concerns and ask important questions, then you must give them a forum in which to practice. And if you want them to seek the best opportunities for themselves and be sure they are valued and respected, they must earn that respect and acknowledgment through their actions and character. None of this can happen as long as you are doing the work for them. In fact, you're sending them the message that you don't believe they're capable of being independent and responsible. And if you don't believe it, why should they?

Lindsey was a good kid who frequently left class without a full understanding of the homework assignment. This became obvious when I graded her work, so I elicited her mother's help to intervene in a constructive way. She explained that she'd been dealing with this problem for most of Lindsey's life and had just about given up the struggle. While I understood her frustration, I knew that no one was winning in this situation, and there was definite room for improvement.

Imagine that you are Lindsey's mom. Lindsey sits down to do her homework and realizes that she doesn't understand the requirements of an assignment. Do you:

- Email or call her teacher to find out what she's supposed to do?

- Email or call her teacher to ask for an extension on the assignment until the directions are made more clear?
- Call your friends whose kids have the same teacher?
- Sit down and look over the assignment yourself to see if you can figure it out?
- Yell at Lindsey and tell her that this is so typical? No matter what, she's on her own—you have washed your hands of this situation.

In all of the above scenarios, you, the parent, are the problem solver or the reminder that your child's efforts are inadequate. Ask yourself what you have just taught Lindsey in handling the situation in one of these ways. Go back to the three goals of raising children who tackle problems, articulate their needs, and take advantage of their opportunities. Has Lindsey met any of these three goals in this scenario? No. In fact, she's performed a double whammy mistake by not paying attention to the assignment when it was given and then allowing the situation to progress to the point that she is now home and still unclear on the expectations. So what should happen in this scenario? I advised Lindsey's mother to have a conversation that went something like this:

Lindsey: Ahhh! I can't do this assignment! I don't understand what the teacher is asking for, and I'm going to mess up and end up with a bad grade if I don't figure this out!

Mom: Okay, back up. You have the assignment sheet in front of you. What does it tell you to do?

Lindsey: It says to complete pages 10 and 11 in the algebraic equations chapter, but we never even went over the material on page 11, so how in the world am I supposed to do this? This is so typical! This teacher never teaches us anything and then expects us to know what to do when we get home.

Mom: So you know the material from page 10?

Lindsey: Well, yeah, I can pretty much do that.

Mom: Great! And I assume that your book comes with explanations and sample equations, and that it goes in some sort of order, from simple to more difficult?

Lindsey: Um, yeah. But she never taught us half of this! It's like she expects us to just figure it out.

Mom: If she expects it, then it's most likely possible. She has taught you the fundamentals, and now it's time to apply those to more difficult problems. I'm sure you can do it.

Lindsey: Yeah, but that will take, like, an hour!

Mom: Good thing your only job is to be a student.

Lindsey: I hate when you say that. And what if I try and still can't figure it out?

Mom: You tell me. What are your options?

Lindsey: I guess I can call Peter; he's pretty good at math. Or I can look for problems that are similar on Google. Worst case, I guess I can ask her about it before school tomorrow, but that means even more time I have to spend at school.

Mom: All good options. I'm going to leave you with something to think about: How can you avoid this same thing happening again in the future? It's worth a few minutes of your time to come up with a plan so you never have to deal with this again. Okay, I'm going to leave you alone. See you when you're finished.

Now, how does this conversation differ from the Mom-stepping-in-to-save-the-day approach? How does it support and encourage Lindsey, rather than convince her that she just can't overcome this weakness? What lessons have been learned, and who has learned them? How will this conversation help your children to grow and mature into responsible adults?

And one final question: Does this response to your children's problems in any way show neglect or a lack of caring? Or does it show thoughtfulness and a desire for your children to take ownership of their own problems? Being a loving parent doesn't mean solving problems for your children. It means helping your children solve their problems themselves. There is certainly nothing wrong with helping children through one problem, for instance, and then stepping back. But be sure to step back.

Please note: At no time did this mom get caught up in the teacher blaming or negativity introduced by the child. She did not join in in assigning blame elsewhere but kept the focus solely on what the child could do to solve the problem. A few conversations like this are all it takes to send a clear message to your children that when they come home unprepared to do what is required of them, it is their responsibility to come up with a solution. You will not allow them to pass the buck, and you will fully expect them to figure it out.

Making Them Take Responsibility

Let's try another scenario. Andrew, a high school senior, receives a zero on a presentation because he was unprepared when called on. He is furious with the teacher and devastated about the impact the zero has had on his grade. Do you:

- Show up at school demanding to see the teacher? You have never seen your child this upset, and the teacher needs to know it.
- Call the principal to demand that your son be given the opportunity to present what he has completed?
- Send him to his room to complete the work that night and present it to the teacher tomorrow?
- Wait a few weeks to see how the grade impacts his overall grade in the class, and then get involved at that point?

- Drill him about why he was unprepared and remind
  him of all the other times he's done something similar?

Again, think about the ramifications of the above actions. What lessons will be taught and learned? Now let's look at a productive way to handle this situation.

Andrew: I can't believe her! She's hated me since day one! Just because I didn't have my presentation ready today, she told me I can't go at all. Now I'm going to end up with a C in this class!

Dad: Whoa. Hold on. What was the due date for this assignment?

Andrew: We were supposed to have everything ready two days ago. But I thought my partner was printing out the materials, and he thought I was doing it. It was an honest mistake, but she still wouldn't let us print out our stuff when she called on us. She kept saying it was supposed to be ready ahead of time. What's the big deal? It would have taken, like, one minute.

Dad: Well, yeah, it would have taken *you* one minute. What if everyone did what you did and waited until class to print?

Andrew: Whatever, it's still unfair. I had the work done, and now I'm not going to get any credit for it.

Dad: It sounds like you have two separate issues here: One, your work was done; two, you didn't have it ready for the teacher so she could actually see your work. In the real world, which you're getting ready for, what would happen?

Andrew: I'm sure my boss would give me time to get it done.

Dad: Really? So no due dates in the real world? No consequences for not meeting deadlines?

Andrew: Okay, maybe, but what about this assignment? I can't just take a zero.

Dad: I agree that just accepting a zero should be your last option. And you need to know that that may be the ultimate result, and you'll have to deal with the consequences if it is. But, yeah, you should spend some time trying to figure out how to solve this problem. Remember, there are always options, and there are always choices. You made one choice in not being prepared, and now you're paying the price. But sometimes you can minimize the damage by thinking through your options. Admitting your mistake and asking if there is anything you can do to remedy it would be a good place to start. And I'd think about some ways you might make up the grade, if your teacher allows it. That way you're prepared to have a conversation that shows you've given this some thought. If you want to run this conversation by me ahead of time, I'd be glad to listen and offer feedback.

Dad retreats to another room of the house and gives Andrew time to think through his problem. He has expressed empathy but also pointed out the obvious—that Andrew has created this problem but that we can often turn problems around if we think through them. He hasn't provided solutions; he's put the onus on Andrew to do that. But he has provided an ear and some guidance to get Andrew back on track, his job as a parent. And that's the key: We do not relinquish our parental responsibilities and leadership when our children become teenagers; we merely wean our growing children of their dependency on us. We teach them how to become their own advocates.

This principle should be applied in all areas of children's lives. In the sports arena, in clubs and activities, in after-school jobs, anywhere children move and interact with others, the message should be one of responsibility for one's own actions. I will discuss this at length in chapter 4, but teenagers will attempt to deflect blame in most situations. They will look for any opportunity to blame coaches, teammates, club members, and employers for their own performance. Want to know a secret? They even blame you. Your children will out you if you write a paper for them or heavily edit their words. They will flat out tell me that you're an engineer and you built their project for them. They will also tell me the opposite—that you're never home and they never get the benefit of parental help like other kids do. They tell me these things because they are trying to deflect the responsibility from themselves to you. And they do the same thing when they blame the other adults in their lives for their problems. Just being aware that they are doing this will help you frame your responses in more productive ways. You will see that partnerships with other adults in your children's lives will aid you in understanding children's motivations and nudge them down the path of independence.

We often don't realize what we haven't taught our children until they are heading off for college. Then it hits us: I never had her do her own laundry so she would know what to do when she gets to college. And did I ever teach him how to fill out a check or balance a checkbook? Does she know the difference between a debit card and a credit card? Thankfully, these lessons are all fairly easily taught on short notice. A brief demonstration or explanation usually suffices. However, teaching responsibility and problem solving is a gradual, lifelong process. At the very least, it must be implemented during the high school years in preparation for college and the real world. If it isn't taught during the high school years, when will it be? I certainly understand parents' hesitation to let their children take a fall. You see high school as eminently important to your children's future, and it is, but you have to keep your eyes on the big picture. If you're honest with yourself, how important was that one chemistry lab grade you earned as a junior? And that one zero you got the night you didn't do your math homework—how is that affecting you now? Do you get the point? It's all relative. But what are not relative are the lifelong lessons learned or not learned in these situations.

Although it might not feel like it right now, your children's lives are not going to be ruined by a single zero on an assignment or one bad grade in a class. Yes, a grade-point average can make the difference between one university admission and another, but even considering that, would attending a second-choice school ruin a student's chances for future success? The point is that academic mistakes in high school generally do not lead to irreversible, life-altering outcomes. But your refusal or reluctance to allow your children to make decisions, learn from consequences, and determine options could absolutely affect them for the rest of their lives. This is one of the many reasons that parenting is so difficult. The easy responses are to throw up your hands or to jump in and save your kids. The difficult response is to let your kids flounder somewhat until they figure it out on their own. The former teaches nothing about character and perseverance; the latter teaches everything. Which will you choose?

CHAPTER 4

Getting Teens to Accept Responsibility for Their Work, Their Decisions, and Their Mistakes

E XCUSES. THE WORLD IS FILLED WITH THEM, AND IT'S really no wonder. Politicians make excuses for their questionable behavior, athletes make excuses for using performance-enhancing drugs, movie stars make excuses for their messy personal lives, and all of them blame the media for reporting the salacious details of their misbehavior.

Making excuses and blaming others has become a national pastime, and teenagers have learned from the best. I have probably heard every excuse out there, and I have watched children blame anyone and everyone if it meant they could delay taking responsibility for their choices or avoid embarrassing themselves.

Social psychologists have found that as human beings, we tend to excuse our own bad behavior but find the same behavior questionable in others. When it comes to our actions, we blame the situation or circumstances in order to justify our behavior, but when others exhibit the same behavior, we readily recognize it as wrong. This is why, in a survey conducted in 2010 by Dr. Susan Krauss Whitbourne, the vast majority of university students who admitted to cheating blamed it on situations out of their control or on the professor.[1] They did not blame it on any laziness on their part. Those same students, however, readily admitted that cheating shortchanges student learning and is wrong. Wrong for others, apparently, but not for themselves.

You can imagine, then, the mentality of students who are even younger and less mature than their college counterparts. Teenagers want their teachers to like them, their parents to be proud of them, and their peers to respect them. If any of those relationships are in jeopardy, most teens will make excuses and blame others to protect their reputations. They care what others think of them, especially parents, teachers, coaches, bosses, religious leaders, and last, but certainly not least, their peers. Put them in a school situation where they have to perform to an expected standard, follow rules, and maintain their popularity among their friends, and it's easy to see why they would make excuses and play the blame game in order to survive. School is like a petri dish of scenarios where one excuse grows into another and the blame keeps multiplying.

If you were to take on the role of Teacher for the Day, you might be surprised at the depth and breadth of excuses you would hear. Imagine that a project is due and it is one minute before the bell rings to start class. You are preparing for class when seven students line up to explain why they don't have their assignments:

Jim: I had to work late last night and didn't get to finish the work.
Neil: My mom is sick, and we didn't get home from the hospital until late.
Melissa: I spent all class period yesterday in the counselor's office and missed your final instructions.

Tanequa: I had a headache and couldn't think.

Maria: I don't have a computer at home, and no one was there to take me to the library.

Dan: I left my flash drive at my mom's house, and I was at my dad's house last night, so I had no way of getting it.

Marcel: Are you kidding me? No way could I get this done last night. There were gunshots outside my window, and my little brother was scared.

If you're thinking this is an exaggeration, it's not. This is a typical day in the classroom anytime an assignment is due. And these aren't the only students unprepared. There is Mickey, sitting quietly in the corner and avoiding eye contact, who won't tell me why he doesn't have his project. There's Emily, who's been struggling with emotional issues and whom I will talk to privately after class. There is Tony, who turns in one page of the four-page assignment and hopes I won't notice, and when I do, explains that he's had play rehearsal every night. The excuses are everywhere, some perfectly valid, some outright lies, most somewhere in between. Imagine trying to discern which are legitimate and which are as genuine as a three-dollar coin. And imagine having to do this while twenty-five other students stand by, waiting.

I didn't walk you through this exercise to garner sympathy or score one for the teachers. I walked you through it so you could see the pervasiveness of excuse making and blaming in a teenager's life. Like adults, they have their own set of demands placed on them daily. They have to be on time for class, they have to follow the varying rules enforced by different teachers, they have to remember deadlines for multiple assignments, requirements, and teacher preferences. There are so many ways they can cut themselves on the sharp edges of any given day that it's not surprising they cushion themselves with excuses and justifications.

The problem, though, is that every time they get a pass as a result of an accepted excuse, it strengthens their resolve to use excuses again. They quickly determine which adults are suckers and which accept no excuses whatsoever. Both extremes only hurt the situation for everyone involved. Most teachers, coaches, and youth leaders try to find middle ground, caring for children as people but still holding them accountable for their behavior and choices. We want them to take responsibility for their decisions and their actions.

I'm betting you want the same.

Parents and Teachers Should Be on the Same Side

Teachers and parents can be incredibly strong allies when it comes to getting kids to take responsibility for themselves. We should never be on opposite sides, because when we are, we are working against the children.

But teenagers will play teachers against parents and parents against teachers, just like they play Mom against Dad, and vice versa. They do this with one very specific and masterful stroke. When students earn a bad grade, the number one excuse they give their parents is that it's the teacher's fault. They may not say it in those exact words, but you might have heard variations of these sentiments:

- My teacher hates me!
- I'm telling you, my teacher is stupid. She makes mistakes all the time!
- That teacher doesn't understand me at all.
- He never explains anything! He's supposed to be the teacher, and he never even teaches us!
- I swear, he hates teenagers.
- My teacher didn't even give us instructions for that assignment. How was I supposed to know what to do??

- That teacher is known for playing favorites. You should see how she treats me compared to the kids she loves.
- She never calls on me.
- He acts like I'm stupid and embarrasses me in front of the class.
- I tried to talk to him about my grade, and he wouldn't even listen to me!
- Everyone told her question 11 was unfair, and she still wouldn't change her mind.
- Ever since I got into trouble that one time, she won't even give me a second chance.
- He's so unfair! He won't accept any late work no matter how hard I tried.

I would bet money that every single one of these statements has been made about me at some point in my teaching career. And every single one of them is, at its foundation, an excuse. It is placing the blame on someone else in order to avoid taking responsibility for one's own actions or inactions. And even if the blame is warranted and the excuse justifiable, it doesn't change the fact that the person making it is unwilling to work within the circumstances presented.

In any situation, we have parameters in which to function. Some students are economically disadvantaged and do not have the technology, brand-name clothes, and fancy cars that their wealthier peers have. These kids eat breakfast and lunch at school, wear the same clothes repeatedly, ride the bus to and from school, and are quite aware that they don't have what other students have. Their stresses don't end when they leave school, either. Many work twenty or more hours a week to help the family pay the bills. They babysit younger siblings and pitch in with chores to ease the burdens of single parents. They have no access to computers and school supplies and must make special arrangements each time they need what their peers have within easy reach.

They can, and do, share this information with teachers in an effort to explain their actions and inactions. Most teachers are sympathetic to these students and do everything they can to help, including using their own money to fund supplies or field trips, pulling from special school funds, extending deadlines, and providing time to use school computers. Free and reduced-price breakfasts and lunches are federally funded and ensure that kids are not hungry so they can function and think clearly. The help is there, but in the end, the children must decide that they can and will overcome their disadvantages. Even in the poorest schools, dedicated teachers are working hard to provide a solid education to students. Even working two jobs, dedicated parents are supporting their kids and encouraging their learning. All the more reason, then, for children to appreciate everyone who comes together to work for them. Kids must then take responsibility for the huge part they play in their own education. Once aid is given to children in need, they should be able to finish assignments, ask for extra help, and advocate for themselves.

Some children have economic advantages but are dealing with family issues that consume their time and lessen their interest in school and other activities. In my experience, family issues are the leading cause of distraction in a teenager's life. These include divorce, siblings with drug problems, physical or emotional abuse, parents with health problems, death of a parent, being shuttled among family members, alcoholism, or even a new baby in the house. Kids will frequently confide in teachers about these issues because they are desperate to talk to someone who isn't involved. Sometimes they share subtly through writing assignments or creative outlets such as artwork or music, hoping the teacher will notice. Other times they approach a teacher and find a way to work their issues into the conversation. If they feel especially close to their teacher, they may completely unload, no holds barred, all of the family secrets spilled.

And sometimes they use their family issues as an excuse to get out of doing their work or to turn it in late. It's a delicate matter, especially when the teacher is fully aware of what's going on at home. It requires us to take a humane approach, but again, we must hold kids accountable, just as you should. While we sympathize with their situation, we have to send the message that life must go on. In fact, school provides a healthy escape for them, a chance to leave the family angst behind and engross their minds in other thoughts and challenges. If teachers and parents can let them know that we understand what they're going through but that we still expect them to meet their obligations, we are teaching them to muddle through and carry on in times of crisis.

So while we must accept that teenagers have very real issues in their lives and some are facing obstacles no one that age should ever have to face, their lives are their reality. They cannot give up hope by being permitted to shut down at school. They must ask for and accept the support they get from teachers, parents, and organizations while also realizing that they alone must ultimately step up and take responsibility for their learning.

When the Excuses Are Manipulative

I like to give kids the benefit of the doubt when it comes to what they tell me. But I've been lied to more times than I can count, and as difficult as it is, sometimes you need to accept the fact that your kids will lie through their teeth to protect their reputations or to cover their tracks.

I have had kids cry to me with elaborate stories about a dying parent or grandparent only to find out that everyone in the family was perfectly healthy. One kid told me his homework was always late because he worked the closing shift at a local fast-food joint.

Turns out, he never held a job at all. In conversations with other teachers, I've discovered that students who claimed to miss my class to talk to them never actually set foot in their classroom. Same goes for students who swore they were at the nurse's office or the counselor's office. Each time it just so happened to be a test or quiz day.

The worst excuses, however, are the ones that involve you, the parents. It's probably been a long time since you've been called out by a teacher, but it's about to happen, so get ready. The most egregious excuses involve absences in which a parent calls a healthy student in sick so the child can avoid a school responsibility. This happens all the time, and no one is fooled. It is pretty obvious when a student is not ready for a test or not prepared to turn in an assignment. We see it coming. So when the due date arrives and the student is absent, it doesn't take a rocket scientist to figure out what is going on. Coaches can attest to the same problem, which is why most have a policy that athletes who miss practice cannot play in the next game. We know that parents will lie or cover up for their kids, thereby making it twice as hard to teach kids to stop giving excuses.

Please understand that many teachers are also parents. We understand that the parent-child relationship trumps just about any other. Like you, we want our kids to know that we have their backs and that we will always support them. It hurts us when our children are facing negative consequences, and we want to spare them, just like you want to spare your kids. But think about what you're supporting in this scenario. You are giving your children permission to make poor choices, then make excuses for those poor choices, then avoid the consequences of those poor choices. To make matters worse, they now have an unfair advantage over others who did not make excuses.

This is bad enough, but there is something even worse. One of the most dangerous parental mistakes is to allow your children to believe they have power over teachers and other authority figures. More than once I have seen teenagers go after a teacher's job or reputation in order to take the heat off themselves and place it on the teacher.

Jeffrey was the King of Excuses. He expended more effort trying to get around work than he would have spent if he had just done the assignment in the first place. He loved to find ways to beat the system and preferred to take a zero rather than endure "another pointless assignment." On a day when a substantial history project was due, Jeffrey showed up empty-handed. The teacher had set up checkpoints along the way to help students complete the project in stages. At each step, Jeffrey had copied work from other students, printed something off the Internet, arranged to be out of class that day, or claimed he didn't understand the assignment. On deadline day, as he watched all the other students turn in their work with sighs of relief, he realized he had to do something. After all, this was a major grade, and a zero would surely cause him to fail the class.

He made every excuse in the book, and the teacher refused to accept any of them. "Jeffrey, you've known all along that this project was due today. You had multiple opportunities to work on this in class and ask for help if you needed it. No, enough is enough. The deadline is the deadline. I'm sorry."

So, with his grade (and in his mind, his entire life) hanging in the balance, he set about shifting the blame to the teacher. He began with his peers, complaining to them about her policies and stirring them up to rebel. During class, he laughed at the teacher's mistakes and got everyone else laughing as well. Other students began to feed off his disruptions, joining him in trying to trip up the teacher.

At home, he took every opportunity to share stories about his teacher's stupidity, lack of clarity, and ridiculous expectations. "You know that zero I got on that project? That was totally her fault. She stumbles all over herself in class, and everyone laughs at her all the time. I can't even understand what she wants us to do with assignments! I'm not the only one either. Everyone thinks she has no business being a teacher. If I had a decent teacher, I'd do so much better in this class."

To back up his claims, Jeffrey attempted to trap the teacher into doing or saying anything that could be used against her. If she joked with students, he took it out of context and insisted that her comments were serious and mean-spirited. His parents, of course, knew nothing about his behavior at school and his ulterior motives. They heard only his side of the story, and given the only information they had, they were appalled at the teacher's apparent incompetence. "We need to get in there to talk to that teacher," they told Jeffrey. "We don't like what we're hearing at all!"

"Don't bother," Jeffrey replied. "It won't do a bit of good. Everyone's parents have already contacted her, and no one ever gets anywhere with her. You're better off talking to someone higher up."

Taking their son at his word, they took their complaints to the principal, the district office, and the school board. The principal went straight to the teacher and questioned her thoroughly. The teacher explained what had really happened in class, assuring her principal that Jeffrey was using her as an excuse for not doing his work.

"I believe you, I really do," he responded. "But these parents are not going to give up. Their son is facing failure in this class, which means he won't graduate on time. They've already contacted the superintendent and the school board, and they are breathing down my neck. Let's give him a chance to do the work. Better late than never, right?"

The teacher had no choice. She was put in a position in which she had to tell Jeffrey that he could make up the history project, and for that matter, all of his other work. She cringed at Jeffrey's smirk. He had won. Her expectations that her students be held accountable and take responsibility for their work had been flouted. Jeffrey passed the course by hastily throwing together missing work and turning it in weeks to months late.

As it turned out, the teacher left at the end of the school year for a completely unrelated personal reason. While Jeffrey had dragged her through the mud, she had privately dealt with her mother's worsening Alzheimer's disease and making decisions about her mother's care. This required her to relocate to another state. Nevertheless, Jeffrey took great pride in the belief that he had single-handedly had his teacher fired. He announced to everyone that she was gone because he had gotten her into trouble. He had conducted an experiment to see if excuses and blaming others would shift the attention away from him. He got his answer.

Jeffrey sounds like a hyperbolic example, and in some ways, he is. But you should know that the various behaviors and excuses he exhibited could be attributed to any number of students who pass through high school doors every day. Your children may have already committed a few of these offenses. Pressed for an excuse, the sweetest kids can behave in ways that would appall their parents. Fortunately, we've figured out as adults that excuses might save us temporarily but will ultimately come back to haunt us. As parents, you want your kids to take responsibility for their work, their decisions, and their mistakes. You can foster this self-actualized behavior in a number of ways:

- When you hear your children give excuses, call them on it. Point it out to them so they know exactly when and how often they are attempting to cover their tracks. Kids jump into self-protection mode and are often unaware that they are making excuses. You can gently ask a series of questions that brings them around to the real reason behind their behavior. Questions like, "How long have you had to do this assignment?" or "What did you do to prepare for the test?" redirect the conversation back to children and force them to reflect on their part in the learning equation.

- The second your children place blame on someone else, stop them and ask them what alternative actions they could have taken. Keep the focus on them, not whomever they are blaming. Through guided discussion, let them come around to the realization that despite others' actions, they are always free to make their own decisions. Every time I call out students on their behavior and they reply with, "But everyone else was talking, too!" I remind them that the only people they are responsible for are themselves. If your children try to blame a friend for their poor behavior, don't let them. Instead, keep the focus on them and help them to discover better, alternative choices.

- Do not let children blame the adults in their lives for their poor decisions unless and until you find that the blame is warranted. You won't know this until you talk to the teacher in question or watch the coach in action, and even then it may take time to get a true picture of the situation. Sometimes letting these adults know that you are monitoring the situation automatically prompts them to take more care with their actions. Talking to teachers and other adults in your children's lives may also provide insight as you discover the two sides to every story.

- Always approach the adults in your children's lives as allies. It is amazing what adults working together can do to help children. The vast majority of teachers, coaches, youth ministers, and club sponsors do what they do because they genuinely love and care about kids. Assume an attitude of cooperation unless they give you a very good reason not to.

- Consistently teach your children that their actions are their own. Empower them to make their own choices and make sure they are fully aware that every decision leads to consequences. Don't suffer the consequences of their decisions for them.

Teaching Your Kids to Make Progress, Not Excuses

I've focused on excuses kids make regarding schooling and academics because this is such an enormous part of their daily lives. But I know that you face excuse making at every turn, so let's discuss what you can do when your children make excuses in their day-to-day home life.

In chapter 1, I shared the psychological motivation behind our willingness or unwillingness to perform tasks. Having an understanding of your children's unique motivational prompts helps tremendously in inspiring them to take action rather than blame others for their inaction. For instance, your expectations that Audrey will feed the dog twice a day must be clearly communicated, and, at least at the onset, a system of checks and balances should be put in place to ensure that Audrey completes that task. She could simply place a note on the dog food that says "Fed" to let everyone know that she has done her job and no one needs to ask her if she remembered (thereby treating her like a child you don't completely trust to be responsible) or nag her (thereby causing her to want to rebel and remind you that she is her own person). Now, if that note does not appear and Spot is checking couch cushions for sustenance, you should simply ask Audrey if she remembered to feed Spot. An excuse the first time a mistake is made is certainly forgivable, but if Audrey is so lax in her responsibility that Spot is now whimpering, the time to accept excuses is over.

At this point, no argument needs to take place. You simply approach Audrey, calmly remind her of her job and the fact that she hasn't been doing it, and let her know that regardless of what else is going on in her life, Spot still needs to eat. She doesn't have a choice in the matter. Like it or not, she has responsibilities to fulfill no matter how busy her life gets. End the conversation on a positive note—"I thank you, and Spot thanks you"—and show complete confidence that Audrey will do as you asked.

If this happens and Audrey is back on board in no time, be sure to acknowledge it and be grateful for her contribution. If, however, she begins to neglect this responsibility again, blaming it on her schedule, or the person who interrupted her, or the fact that it's not even her dog and she never wanted it in the first place, do not—I repeat, do not—engage in a battle of the wills. The absolute worst action you can take when your children make excuses is to get sucked into their excuse making. It's a lose-lose proposition that will infuriate you, exhaust you, and eventually weaken your resolve. Teenagers know this. That's why they do it.

So what do you do? You refuse to listen to it. I'm not talking about a legitimate reason that deserves to be heard. I'm talking about the nonsensical scrambling kids do when they know they blew it and try to cover their tracks. You can immediately discern which one you're dealing with by listening to the first minute or two of their explanation. And you can control whether or not you hear the real reason by asking the right question from the start. Begin by looking them in the eyes and calmly saying, "I will listen to you explain why you haven't been feeding Spot, but I will not listen to any excuse that involves other people. I want to hear what is going on with *you* that is preventing you from feeding the dog. If you start to blame other people, that will be the end of the conversation. But if you keep the focus on you, I will hear you out."

It will take some kids several of these conversations before they will learn that you mean what you say. And you have to mean it. You have to follow through just as you said you would. If they begin to blame others for their lack of responsibility, redirect the conversation back to their behavior. If they continue despite your reminder, end the conversation immediately and explain that you will take away privileges until they are willing to spend the thirty seconds necessary to feed the dog. They won't like it, and that's okay. They are part of a family, and that means that they contribute, and they will learn that when they do, their life is better. But I cannot be emphatic enough about this: You must refuse to engage in the blame game. When your kids understand that Mom and Dad recognize the difference between legitimate reasons and deflecting excuses, they will give up, or at least relent, and begin to take ownership of their choices.

With my own children, I practiced what I preach, and my kids quickly realized that blaming others got them nowhere. It eventually got to the point that if my kids began to shift the blame, I simply held up my hand and shook my head. They stopped midsentence and knew it was pointless to go on. Before long, it became much easier to just own up to what they didn't do and remedy the situation. I can't tell you how much more peaceful and calm our home became when we reached that landmark. Sure, we still argued and annoyed each other, but we didn't yell and scream and slam doors in frustration, because we didn't let conversations escalate to that point. It takes two to tango, and you, the adult, must refuse to enter the dance.

When you find yourself in a battle of the wills with your children and they are handing you every excuse in the book, step back, take a breath, and recognize the situation for the exercise in frustration that it is. It is pointless. It will get you nowhere. No one will win. Refuse to engage any further. Tell your children that the conversation is over until they are willing to speak only of their own behavior and thinking process that led to that behavior. Once they do this, you can help them find a solution that works for everyone. If Audrey explains that she keeps forgetting to feed the dog because she is in a rush to get to school in the morning, the simple solution is for her to set her alarm five minutes earlier. If she doesn't want to do that, she can leave a reminder note on the door so feeding the dog is the last thing she does before heading to school. She should come up with the solution so she is invested in the process. But the solution should not involve your reminders or nagging or long-term negative reinforcement. That very phrase—*long-term negative reinforcement*—doesn't even make sense. The minute negative reinforcement reaches long-term status is the minute you discover that it isn't working.

Reinforcements must be quick and immediate so children tie their behavior to the consequences. A negative reinforcement that doesn't seem to bother a child at all—for instance, you take away video games and your teenager just replaces that diversion with TV watching—is not an effective reinforcement. You must know your children and what is important to them, and you must use negative reinforcement sparingly when discussions and expectations are unproductive. If you treat your teenagers like emerging adults, speaking to them with the confidence that they are capable of doing whatever you ask, teaching them to take responsibility for their own actions, and guiding them through solutions, chances are good that you can employ negative reinforcements much more sparingly.

I would like to include a positive scenario that acknowledges the teenagers who readily admit when they've made mistakes and poor decisions and who blame no one but themselves. It's rare, even for adults, but those kids are out there. They are overwhelmingly polite, respectful, and mature, and they know exactly who they are. They are the kinds of kids who set the standard for character and who, I know, must make their parents incredibly proud. Here's an illustration of just such a kid:

It was the second week of school, and the students had an assignment to write an original poem on a personal theme. I had explained to them that it was my chance to get to know them as people and their chance to express themselves. Since the assignment was creative and dubbed "fun" by the kids, they didn't gripe about the due date. In fact, it seemed that many of them recognized this first assignment as a chance to make a great first impression. Therefore, all the assignments were turned in on time—except for one. I didn't even know that Ryan hadn't turned in his assignment and wouldn't have realized it until I had completed the grading. But that didn't stop him from admitting it to me after class.

"Dr. D., can I talk to you for a minute? I want you to know that I didn't turn in the assignment today. I know, I know, there's really no excuse. There was no reason for me not to get this done, and I'm really disappointed in myself for not doing it. I want you to know that this is not who I am. I am normally a hard worker, and I realize that this makes a very bad first impression. I hope that you won't judge me too harshly and that you'll give me a chance to show you who I really am. I apologize for not taking this assignment seriously. It won't happen again."

I didn't say a word. I couldn't, with my mouth hanging open. Once I found my voice, I assured Ryan that everyone makes mistakes and that I was sure he would work hard and get the assignment to me the next day. I thanked him for his honesty and forthrightness and sent him on his way.

Ryan did prove to me that he was a hard worker, but really,

that was secondary to demonstrating to me what a fine young man he was. You can raise your children to be just like Ryan, but it will take consistent practice in avoiding the blame game and in teaching kids that they are the only ones responsible for their behavior.

What to Do When a Teacher Is Legitimately Ineffective

In this chapter, I have discussed normal classroom situations and the teachers you will likely encounter during your teenagers' high school years. I would be remiss if I did not acknowledge the possibility of dealing with teachers who are past the date at which they should have retired or who chose the wrong profession and are making kids miserable in the process. They exist, and I don't blame you one bit for wanting your kids out of their classrooms. To determine if your children's comments are not just excuses but real concerns about an ineffective teacher, take these steps. Once you do, you will have much stronger legs on which to stand if you have to fight for a teacher's removal:

- When your children complain, hear them out. If you feel their criticisms are warranted, insist that *they* speak to the teacher first. Whether they are frightened freshmen or bold seniors, it is not too early for them to learn to advocate for themselves.

- Encourage them to advocate for themselves by approaching the teacher (or any authority figure) with respect while ensuring that student concerns are voiced and misconceptions are cleared up. When teens leave these conversations, their worries should be alleviated and their questions should be answered.

- If, after the student-teacher conversation, the situation does not improve, then it is time for parents to contact the teacher. Sometimes an email exchange is all that is needed. I would start there unless you are truly alarmed about a specific incident and think a sit-down is necessary. Teachers appreciate having the time to reflect on parent emails and respond after thoughtful consideration. Plus, while their school schedules are tight, making it difficult to talk on the phone, they can respond to email from home or when they can grab a few minutes of uninterrupted time.

- If email doesn't help resolve the situation, your next step is a one-on-one conference with the teacher. Your children should attend the meeting if there is a huge discrepancy between what you are hearing from them and what the teacher is telling you. It's important to get everyone involved in the same room so everyone is hearing the same thing. At this point, you will notice if the teacher appears to be hedging, if there is tension between the two, or if the teacher's words and actions really are unclear or disconcerting.

- If the conference leaves issues unresolved or raises even more red flags, your next step is to get another school official involved. This can be your children's guidance counselor or the department chair, depending on the issue. If it's academic, contact the department chair and tell him the steps you, your children, and the teacher have taken. If it's emotional or behavioral, contact the counselor and explain the situation. These professionals will advocate on your behalf, talk to your children and the teacher separately, and help to work out an amicable solution. They will also take the situation higher if they recognize that the teacher is in the wrong, involving the administration if necessary.

If the situation gets no better, it is now time to contact the principal, armed with evidence of all of the attempts you have made before resorting to contacting the leader of the school. The principal has the authority to move your children into another classroom and to pursue a remediation or termination process with the teacher if the situation warrants it. It is very, very rare for one parental complaint to get a teacher fired, but don't think that your input won't make a difference. You don't know if twenty other parents have already complained about this same teacher, and yours may be the final straw that removes a teacher who really needs to go.

CHAPTER 5

How to Get the Most from Parent-Teacher Conferences and Open Houses

THERE ARE REASONS WHY SOME PARENTS AVOID SCHOOL functions and others are drawn to them with eagerness and excitement. One reason has to do with parents' own experiences in high school; the other has to do with parents' worries about how their children are doing.

Just like your childhood has affected you in more ways than you probably care to recognize, your past experiences with school can color your current viewpoint. If you have fond memories of your high school experience, were a decent student, and liked most of your teachers, you probably have no problem attending conferences and open houses for your children. For you, school is a pleasant place where learning is taking place, adults are supporting students, and memories are being made. It's a fond trip down memory lane to see the all-familiar lockers, sit in student desks, and get reports from teachers.

If your memories are not quite so quaint and school was, in fact, a wholly negative experience, you probably have no desire to return. You remember teachers who disciplined, indoctrinated, and demeaned. Maybe you felt like a social outcast or were unable to learn in the expected way. If school made you feel stupid, it's not surprising that you wouldn't want to return, even twenty-five years later when you have your own high-school-age kids.

The second reason you might avoid returning to the scene of the crime is that you're worried sick about your children's progress or behavior in school. What might teachers tell you that you don't want to hear? Will they make the same comments you've heard from every former teacher, thereby drawing attention to all of your children's weaknesses? It's easy to see why one-on-ones with teachers can be intimidating or feel like a frustrating waste of time. But these opportunities can provide invaluable information about your kids that can help you support them in having a positive high school experience.

Meeting the Teachers

Your first opportunity to get to know your children's teachers is likely the annual open house, generally held in September. The purpose of the open house is to give you a brief introduction to the teachers and their courses. That's it. It's not a time to talk to teachers about your children or to have any sort of conference. It is a quick walk through your children's schedule just so you can see what their day is like. But that doesn't mean it does not have value. I recommend that you pay attention to the following:

- **Each teacher's overall personality.** Is she strict or laid back? Enthusiastic or staid? Open and warm or reserved? You can help your children tremendously in understanding their teachers by sharing your observations with them, and you can tailor your future communications based on the personalities you witnessed.

- **What each teacher stresses as important.** In only ten minutes, you should be able to glean what each teacher values most. Again, share that with your children. "I only spent a short amount of time with him, but boy was it clear that he expects homework to be turned in on time," is all you need to say to reinforce the expectations. Kids are not always as observant as adults, and they can benefit from your perceptions.

- **How the teacher prefers to be contacted.** Most teachers will share this information during open house, and most prefer email since they are rarely in a position to take phone calls during the school day. Email is also the perfect venue for reflecting on what you want to say or ask, with the added benefit that it is documentation of "conversations" with teachers.

When given the opportunity to ask questions at an open house, you should ask if there is anything parents can contribute to the classroom, whether it be time, resources, or boxes of tissues. Teachers remember and appreciate parents who offer a helping hand, and it sets a great precedent of teamwork and support for the school year. In addition, ask any general questions that will help all the parents help their children, such as what tests look like and how students can study best or how much homework students should be doing at night.

Keep in mind that this event offers a brief first impression, one that may not be entirely accurate. But you will definitely know more coming out of open house than you knew going in, so you should find it to be a valuable use of your time. Additionally, your children will see you taking the time to visit their school and meet their teachers. You are saying to your teen, "You may be older and think you don't need me to be involved in your schooling anymore, but I'm going to be there, all through high school, doing whatever I can to support you by staying in contact with your teachers." They may not always appreciate that message; nevertheless, it's an important one to send.

While open houses give you a glimpse into teacher personalities and class expectations, parent-teacher conferences provide a more in-depth look into your teenager's work habits and school personality. It's the difference between scanning a newspaper's headlines and photos, and stopping to thoroughly read the article that interests you most. Built into the annual school calendar, conferences are available for any parents who want to sign up, and they provide personal feedback on students. This is your chance to ask questions, discuss concerns, share successes, or just listen to what each teacher has to say about your children. Because conference schedules usually allow for only ten-to-twenty-minute time slots, you will want to arrive with a plan in order to maximize your time.

We are going to examine four scenarios involving parents who do not take full advantage of these conferences. See if you recognize yourself in these examples. The four scenarios involve:

1. Parents only interested in trying to catch their kids doing something wrong
2. Parents who bring their own issues into the meeting instead of focusing on their children's issues
3. Parents who bring their children to the meeting, destroying the point of the whole exercise
4. Parents who come to the conference just to hear how great their kids are doing and what a great job they've done as parents

In each of these sketches, the parent-teacher conference was not what it should or could have been. The conversations were one-sided, off track, ill focused, or shut down right from the beginning. If we dissect each scenario, we will find where the conversation headed into negative or tangential territory.

Parents Trying to Catch Their Kids Doing Something Wrong

The man walked into my classroom for his scheduled appointment. I greeted him with a smile and a handshake; he greeted me with a frown and a grunt. When he didn't start the conversation or ask any questions about his daughter, Amy, I began discussing her progress up to that point using a printout of her grades. He interrupted me.

"What's this C on this assignment?"

"It was a class assignment on word problems. Amy struggled a bit associating the presented scenarios to the math problems we'd been doing in class, but she seems to have a much better grasp on the concept now."

"Yeah, but she's not allowed to get Cs. She knows that. I'll be talking to her about this tonight and she's going to have to explain this."

I quickly assessed the situation and knew I needed to focus on the positive with this dad. I was about to talk about Amy's strengths and some of the strides she had made in class when he asked, "What about her behavior? Does she give you any trouble?"

"No, Amy's very respectful and kind."

"Well, we've been working on that at home. She talks too much in class. I tell her all the time . . ." and he launched into a story about the one or two times a teacher had described Amy as chatty, her subsequent punishment at home, and the fact that they would enforce it again if any teacher told them she was talking too much.

At this point our time together was almost up. While I found

Amy to be a pleasant, hard-working student, I had barely had time to mention that. Dad had focused on one isolated grade and had inquired about a behavior issue that didn't exist, at least in my class. I was about to try a different tack when my next parent appeared at the door. I thanked Amy's dad for coming. He left with a frown and a grunt.

This first example involves parents who approach conferences as means to bust their teenagers. These "gotcha" parents expect to hear that their children are lazy, and they want teachers to know that they have nothing to do with it. They vent their frustration before they've even been told there's a problem. In an effort to appear supportive of teachers, they attempt to create an us-versus-them relationship in which teachers and parents bond over their mutual dislike for those unbearable teens.

I get it. I really do. Teens can be downright infuriating. As a teacher, I never mind when parents acknowledge this with a wink and a smile. This lends itself more to a tongue-in-cheek "I feel your pain" and "Hang in, brother" kinship that can be enjoyable for parents and teachers alike. It can also make communication more effective down the road when a positive relationship has already been established. I also don't mind when parents point out their kids' weaknesses as a means to solicit validation, advice, or even disagreement. Everyone wants to know what other people think of their kids, and I see nothing wrong with gentle prodding in that direction. "I've been told Jake can be a bit of a class clown," opens the door to conversation about just that, without conveying a defeatist, "My mind's already made up, and Jake clearly takes after his wannabe comedian father" tone.

But this is different. This is fully expecting the worst from children and then distancing yourself as much as possible from the people they have become. I understand the need to convey wonderment at a teenager's personality or work habits: "His mom and I have both worked two jobs his entire life, and now we can't even get him to do a small homework assignment. I swear, he wasn't raised that way." I hear this all the time, and it makes perfect sense for parents to voice this. Their children are reflections of them, and they do not want anyone to be misled into believing that because their children are lazy, they must be lazy.

Amy's dad, however, never gave Amy a chance to prove herself. Instead, he ignored what she had done well and focused only on the one C Amy had earned. When he stated that Amy is "not allowed to get Cs" he revealed way more about himself than he did about his daughter. What he told me was that in his house, little to no consideration is given to individual learning ability, the recognition that everyone has academic strengths and weaknesses, or the allowance that there is a process one must take to achieve mastery, and that process usually involves stumbling along the way. He didn't accept the fact that grades reflect the process of learning, including the times when kids miss the mark.

In addition, he didn't want to "waste time" on his daughter's accomplishments when he was sure there was plenty to find wrong. That's why he shifted the topic to Amy's behavior and introduced the idea that she talks too much, something that hadn't even occurred to me. I can't say if this information affected my attitude toward Amy, but the seed had been planted that she was a talker. Her father had painted her in a negative light, thereby taking the risk that I would follow suit. Was that beneficial to anyone? Was it fair to Amy? She had done nothing to draw such scrutiny.

What was perhaps more upsetting to me was thinking about what would take place at home. Amy would be called out about that one C. She would learn that mistakes are not growing experiences but something to be ashamed of. She would discover that the almighty grade would always hold court over a love of learning and a desire to improve. This is exactly the kind of mentality and pressure that leads children to cheat, copy homework, or plagiarize papers. The love of learning disappears when all anyone cares about is a letter on a report card.

Also, Amy would learn that she cannot escape her past mistakes. Talking a little too much a few times when she was younger would be thrown in her face repeatedly. She would not be given a reprieve; in fact, she would be expected to repeat her mistakes and never grow out of them. Imagine the confusion in Amy's household. On one hand, she is expected to achieve near perfection academically. On the other hand, she is expected to repeat the same behavioral mistakes ad infinitum. Where is the logic in this argument?

Parents with Their Own Issues

Two parents walked into my room looking upset. They sat down, eager to hear about their daughter's work in my class, but the tension was palpable.

Mom spoke up first. "We're curious as to how Maddie is doing in your class. Does she seem okay to you?"

Dad rolled his eyes in disgust. "For God's sake, Mary, how many times do I have to tell you she's fine?! Give the girl a break!"

Mom explained, "It's just that we're going through a divorce, and she's having a really hard time with it, and—"

"You know what?" Dad interjected. "She'd be fine if you quit bringing it up every five minutes and asking her if she's fine." Turning to me, he said, "I bet she's fine at school, right? I bet you'd never even know what was going on with us if my wife didn't just tell you."

"Um, well, Maddie is doing okay." I was hedging, not wanting to add to the tension. "She has seemed a little quiet lately, and this might explain it."

"I knew it!" Mom yelled at Dad. "What did I tell you? I know her better than you do."

Dad seethed in anger as I assured them both that I would keep an eye on Maddie and alert them if I saw any reason for concern. I rushed through her academic progress in the little time remaining, and both parents left glaring at one another. I'm not sure that they had heard a word I'd said about their daughter's academics.

This next type of parents who approach conferences with mindsets that may stand in the way of true productivity are the ones who bring their own issues into meetings. These parents are grappling with difficult personal issues that they allow to overshadow their focus on their children.

Maddie's parents are going through a divorce. They are attending parent-teacher conferences together, so it appears, at least on the surface, that they are able to put their differences aside to concentrate on their daughter's interests. Sometimes that is exactly the case, and it is admirable. I have great respect for adults who are always parents first. Unfortunately, sometimes parents engage in a battle of one-upmanship, each trying to prove to be the better parent, each blaming the other for the divorce, each spending all their conference time airing their dirty laundry rather than learning about their children.

This is truly sad. The fact of the matter is that yes, Maddie is hurting, whether she openly demonstrates that to me or not. Yes, she is aware that her parents blame one another for the current state of affairs. Yes, she would be utterly humiliated if she knew her parents were fighting in front of her teachers. Yes, she wants them to put all that aside and pay attention to her needs during conference time. Yes, she deserves that.

I'm not unsympathetic. I have plenty of divorced family members and friends, and I've seen how it tears people apart. If you fall into this category, talk to your friends, work through it with a counselor, pray with your pastor, commiserate with other people in the same situation—do whatever it takes to heal. But don't bring your personal battles into conferences that are designed to focus on your children. Should you mention that you're going through a divorce and worried about your child? Absolutely, if you feel comfortable divulging that information. But your only concern should be making sure that your children are coping and that their school life isn't being negatively affected by what's going on at home. If you ask them to, teachers will be especially watchful for signs of distress and can alert you immediately if they see something of concern. They can also recommend visits with the school counselor or be more conscientious and sensitive about their comments to students.

There are wide-ranging benefits to sharing this kind of information with the people who spend eight hours a day with your children. Teachers welcome candid conversations that help us do our jobs better. But no good comes from listening to parents verbally duke it out during a conference—except maybe sympathy for their children. The only message you send when you fight over who has damaged your children more is that both of you are in a dead heat for first place. I'm not denying the pain either of you feels or your need to vent your anger, but there is a time and a place, and a parent-teacher conference isn't it.

Parents Who Bring Their Children to Conferences

I was relieved when I saw that Alex's parents had signed up for a conference. Although Alex was a nice young man, he did not work to his potential. Alex was a sensitive kid, and I knew that if I approached him with my thoughts, he would misinterpret my concern for not liking him. He was the kind of kid who needed to know he was liked and who did not take constructive criticism well. It was the perfect situation for a brief conference where I could run my concerns by his parents in confidence and see if we could work together to encourage Alex's efforts.

When I walked to the door to greet Alex's parents, there stood Alex, smiling. He accompanied his parents into the room.

"So Alex, you came to parent conferences," I said, hoping he would explain.

"Yep," he acknowledged, still smiling.

Immediately, I felt stifled. My opportunity to speak to Alex's parents confidentially had just flown out the window; now I would need to schedule another conference.

This type of parents who don't get the most from conferences are those who bring along their children so that they, too, can hear what the teachers have to say. Now, if you pay attention, schools specify their intentions for these meetings by the title they give them. If your children's school refers to them as parent-teacher-student conferences, then the intention is for children to be an active part of the discussion. Those conferences are quite different, though, from the standard parent-teacher conferences that most of us attend each year. These are designed expressly for parents and teachers. That's it. The intention is for both parties to speak frankly about the children, something that often can't or won't happen if the children are sitting right there listening.

I'm sure you've had conversations about your children that you wouldn't want them to hear, especially in their teenage years. You've talked to your mother about her granddaughter's choice of boyfriends. You've swapped stories with friends about the stupid, inexplicable things your kids have done. You've whispered to your spouse about your son's lack of motivation and plotted ways to extract him from the couch.

You get the point. They don't need to hear everything we have to say about them. The same applies in parent-teacher conferences. Teachers want to be frank with you, and they want you to be honest with them. They don't want to have to tiptoe around their students' feelings—they already do that five days a week.

They want to work with you as partners and will feel much freer to be honest with you if the children in question are out of earshot. So if you really want to know what's going on with your kids, leave them at home and let the teachers tell you.

Now let's look at a fourth scenario that may not seem to be a problem on the surface but perhaps needs a little reevaluation on the part of the parents.

Parents of Nearly Perfect Kids

I greeted Stan's parents., who were polite and eager to hear about Stan's performance in my class. We began promptly with a review of his grades.

"Well, Mr. and Mrs. C.," I chuckled. "This is one of those easy conferences where I have very little to say. I know that you check Stan's grades online so you're aware that he has a 98 in my class."

They both nodded happily.

"So as you can see, he obviously grasps all of the content, works very hard, and maintains exceptional grades. He is a joy to have in class and is truly a model student."

They nodded again, smiling, and then Mr. C. asked, "Where is Stan in the class ranking?"

I concentrated on keeping the smile on my face. "We don't have a class ranking. I tell the kids that the only people they are competing with are themselves. They should be looking for improvement in their own work."

"Okay, then, what can he do to improve?"

I didn't have the first clue what to say. The kid had a 98! So I shifted gears and talked about upcoming assignments and what he might do to prepare for those. Mr. and Mrs. C. were happy for the heads up and thanked me for all I do for their son.

This final example consists of parents who have great kids

and know it. Like all parents, they view their children as a reflection of them, so they are understandably proud that their kids are academic achievers. No doubt these parents are actively involved in their children's learning, regularly monitor their grades, and continually push them to do better. In many ways, they are ideal parents. What could possibly be wrong with parents who have raised hard-working, high-achieving kids?

Nothing, as long as they don't use parent-teacher conferences to bask in the glory of their great parenting. You may be guilty of this if you see every single one of your children's teachers on the night of conferences and sit quietly, expecting a tide of compliments to wash over you. You have no questions, no concerns, really, no reason for being there. You know your children's averages, and you know that the only improvement would require perfection, so you don't really have a legitimate cause for taking one of the coveted parent-teacher conference time slots.

Before you get too angry at me for making this statement, hear me out. There are parents out there—plenty of them—who really need to be sitting in those conferences. They are working multiple jobs that keep them away from home, and they count on that time to learn about their kids. They are facing family turmoil and are desperate to know if their children are showing signs of stress. They have real academic concerns and are worried that their children are failing. Their children have come home crying over social issues on more than one occasion, and it is breaking their hearts. They have problems, and they need answers. They are usually the last to find the time to sign up for conferences, and by the time they do, every slot is taken, some by the parents who have kids who are almost perfect.

Do you see the problem? All too often, the parents who don't need to be there are, and the parents who desperately need and want to be there can't find any availability. Yes, they can always request a conference on another day, but many won't. They're tired, or they're hoping the problem will remedy itself, or they don't want to impose, or . . . Reasons and excuses come easily when they have to take the initiative rather than having an opportunity presented to them.

If you're a parent of a stellar student, you're probably wondering how any of this is your problem. Perhaps you're thinking that your kids are doing better because of the effort you put into raising them, including reserving a time for conferences as soon as you can, and you're probably right on many fronts. Even if you don't feel anything for parents who really need time with the teacher, my question for you is, What do you hope to gain from the conference? If it's more good news, validation of you as a parent, and the beauty of hearing wonderful things about your children, I don't fault you. But I do ask you to reconsider. You know you have great kids. Revel in it. Let people tell you, but don't take up time that can be used to really help a kid who needs it.

If your answer is that no matter how well your children are doing, they can always do better, then I applaud your drive. In this case, come armed with specific questions directed at getting to the bottom of what kinds of learners your children are. Ask for tangible strategies for success that you can employ at home. If your children are doing exceptionally well in a particular class, ask that teacher what works for your children and share that with the other teachers. Additionally, be prepared to share information with teachers about how they might engage your children, extend their learning, challenge them, and provide opportunities for them to grow. I love having these conversations with parents because it shows that they care about learning and striving to be better, not just the number grade on the report card.

The point is that if you have a legitimate reason for being there, by all means go. But if you're honest with yourself and can admit that it just makes you feel good, don't go. Your time would be better served having a great dinner with your children and telling them how proud you are of them. And the teachers' time will be better served talking to parents who would do anything to be in your shoes.

How to Reap the Benefits of Conferences

Now that you know what *not* to do, it's time to talk about what *to* do to make the most of your time with your children's teachers. Your goal is to discover information about your children that will help you to understand them better. It follows that this information will help you to better work with them at home so they can find success at school. Your other goal may be to share information that would be helpful to the teacher. This can include personal revelations, past academic experiences, testing outcomes, personality nuances, or outside interests that might serve as motivational tools. If you have specific questions to ask or specific knowledge to share, you should schedule a conference. If you have no concerns, no questions, or nothing in particular to share that may help your children, you probably don't need to be there.

In the first scenario, we had a father who was still holding his daughter accountable for behavior she hadn't exhibited in at least a year. He had a low opinion of her effort, and he conveyed that with no concern about how it might sway teachers' opinions of his daughter. In order to avoid this, remind yourself of the power of suggestion. Do not put negative ideas about your children into teachers' heads. Extend the same forgiveness you would hope for if you had made poor choices in the past. Remind yourself that this is the first time these particular teachers have encountered your children, and they will draw their own conclusions based on what they witness. Your children may have outgrown their bad habits or may be working hard to beat them. Help them. Don't be the constant reminder of last year's F or sophomore year's multiple detentions. Just listen. If there is a problem, the teachers will let you know.

If you'd really like to cut to the chase and find out if Amy is being disruptive, frame the question in a nonaccusatory way. "How are Amy's listening skills, and does she pay attention?" There. You've asked without insinuating anything. Now you'll get an honest answer that isn't swayed by bias.

If you recognized yourself as a parent with your own issues from the second example, don't beat yourself up. What's done is done, but there's always another day. No one can fault you for being caught up in emotions and letting them get the best of you. The fault is earned, however, if you let it stand in your way of being a good parent. If you can't stand to be in the same room with your ex, then don't come to conferences together. Either split up and see different teachers or decide which one of you will attend. If you are able to put aside your differences for an hour or so, come and learn about your children together.

Start by letting the teachers tell you what they want to tell you. If they have seen a change in Maddie, they will likely bring it up and ask if you know anything about the cause. They've opened the door, and you can walk right in. If you decided ahead of time that you would broach the subject with teachers, decide also who will do the talking and what will be said. The situation doesn't have to be horribly awkward, nor should it be. You might say something like this:

"I'm not sure if Maddie has said anything, but her father and I are getting a divorce. We are trying mightily to minimize the effects on Maddie, so we wanted to ask if you've noticed any changes in her behavior or in her work."

One sentence, and it's out there. You've begun a civilized conversation that will get you exactly the information you want as well as alerted the teachers to possible problems down the road. This is different from putting unfair ideas in teachers' heads, as I mentioned earlier. If you have cause to worry about how a personal problem is affecting your children, you should convey that to teachers. The general rule of thumb is to share information that can help your children be safe, secure, and successful. Withhold information that serves no constructive purpose. Decide this before you walk in the door, or you will find yourself going off on tangents that waste precious conference minutes.

The correct way to handle the third scenario pretty much speaks for itself: Don't bring your kid to the parent-teacher conference!

In our fourth scenario, we had the stellar student with a 98 average. I explained why this conference is likely unnecessary, but if you firmly believe in meeting all of your children's teachers face-to-face, there are ways to benefit from these conferences. Rather than asking how your children can improve, ask what they can do to extend their learning and challenge themselves. Teachers have a plethora of resources at their disposal and can usually make recommendations for further study or exploration. For instance, I had a student who was an exceptional writer and had a very high average in my class. Her parents came prepared to ask me how I felt about her writing and if I thought she was talented enough to turn it into a career down the road. This led to discussions about writing contests and camps with which she could become involved. Based on our conversation, I began funneling contest information her way and asking her about her writing outside of class. I later provided a reference for her to an honors writing camp, all because of this short conversation with her parents. The key is to have a purposeful mission when you attend conferences and know what you want to accomplish with each teacher.

Do You Need a Private Conference?

Finally, ask for a private conference outside of the scheduled school conferences if you cannot accomplish your goals in the allotted time. Issues that will probably require more time include:

- Children who are having serious academic problems that go beyond an assignment or two. This warrants a deeper look into what is going on and a more studied approach to finding solutions. If your children are doing poorly in a class, don't seem to grasp concepts, and are getting further and further behind, you should schedule time with the teacher.

- Social issues with peers that can't be solved by changing seats or resolving a minor issue. Let the teacher know in advance that your child is having issues, give the teacher a chance to monitor and try to remedy them, and if the situation doesn't improve, schedule an appointment.

- Personality conflicts with the teacher that will need to be resolved for the student to have academic success. This includes various grading discrepancies or questions on multiple assignments, words that have been exchanged that are causing the student to give up or retreat to a corner, or self-esteem issues brought on by the teacher's actions. Sometimes teachers just need to know that you are aware and watching, and they will be more careful about what they say and do. Sometimes teachers have no idea how a student feels and are dismayed to discover that there is tension they didn't know existed. I had a student whom I liked enough to joke around with and occasionally tease, thinking all the while that her smiles and laughter were genuine. And all the while, she was just holding it in until she got home and cried to her mother. I was stunned when I discovered that she thought I didn't like her and was picking on her. You better believe I changed my behavior after that.

- Concerns about learning disabilities or emotional issues. These definitely warrant a longer period of time, and it can be beneficial to invite counselors, special education teachers, or social workers to the meeting. This will bring all of the professionals together to assess the situation, determine if testing is needed, or just allay parental fears about their children. I recommend that you first provide information via email as to your concerns; then the appropriate people can plan to attend.

- Anger at the teacher about anything. We tend to get quite emotional about our kids, especially when we feel they've been wronged. Please don't enter a conference with the intention of pointing fingers and demanding immediate results. Remember that there are two sides to every story, and one side is coming from a teenager. Anger rarely accomplishes anything but producing more anger. I remember a mom who pointed her finger in my face and threatened to go straight to the principal if I didn't round her daughter's grade up on the last day of school. There was nothing about her actions, tone of voice, or approach that led me to believe I could work with her. I encouraged her to go to the principal, and when she did, pointing that same finger, he saw the situation for what it was and ushered her out the door. Irrational, irate parents don't get anywhere with teachers and administrators. Instead, schedule a conference when you have cooled off and are able to listen and keep an open mind.

SOME FINAL DO'S AND DON'TS

Do listen to what the teacher is saying, both outright and between the lines.

Don't jump in to defend your children or minimize their behavior. A three-hundred-pound student with a bad reputation threatened my life, and when I conferenced with his mother, her response was, "Oh, Leroy wouldn't hurt a fly!" Let's just say that her assurance didn't do much to assure me.

Do share your insights into your kids' personalities, what works for them, and what doesn't. Teachers recognize parents as their greatest source of information when it comes to children, so please share anything that you think would be of help.

Do understand that some teachers and kids don't click and may never like each other, but . . .

Don't accept a teacher who hurts feelings or is unfair.

Do follow up at home with your own repercussions for poor behavior or lack of effort. I've had parents take away cell phones until they hear from me that behavior or effort have improved.

Don't expect the teachers to handle every problem on their own. We count on your reinforcement.

Do let teachers and children know that you will check back in two weeks. This keeps everyone accountable and shows your commitment to long-term solutions.

Do listen to what all your children's teachers say in order to get the big picture. One teacher may not be able to provide a truly accurate portrait of your children.

Do verbalize to teachers what your children tell you about their classes. Check for discrepancies, especially in regard to the focus of study or class expectations. Be sure that your children know what's important for each class.

Don't ask how your children are doing in comparison to other children. Teachers cannot discuss other children with you, and it really doesn't matter where they rank anyway. What matters is how they are doing as individuals and if they are growing as learners. You can ask, "Is Bobby meeting all of the standards? Is he where he should be?" and that should elicit the information you are looking for.

Do remember the role you play in your children's education. You are support systems, partners with teachers, enforcers, and role models. It's a fine line to walk, but I'm confident you can do it.

CHAPTER 6

Homework and Extracurriculars: Should You Still Be Involved in High School?

I T'S HARD TO ARGUE WITH OVER FIFTY STUDIES, ALL CON-ducted in recent years, and all stating that parental involvement is the single most important factor in school success. All of the findings suggest that when parents invest in their children's education, grades improve, attitudes improve, behavior improves, and teachers improve. It seems like a win-win situation, but it's actually a precarious one, especially at the high school level.

The famous tightrope-walking Wallendas have nothing on the balancing act it takes to parent teenagers. It may be trite, but it's true: parents walk a fine line, during these years, between holding on and letting go. Involvement in school requires an especially fine-tuned relationship in which parents continue to provide support and guidance while at the same time placing greater responsibility and trust in their children.

As a yoga enthusiast, I've found that the practice instills philosophies that are applicable well beyond the yoga mat. If you've ever tried to master a challenging pose, you know what it takes: flexibility, strength, focus, and perfect balance. And truly, parenting requires the exact same skills. Just as in yoga, the balance doesn't happen overnight. It takes years of strengthening, holding on, correcting, overcorrecting, bumbling, crashing, and starting over again. If you're lucky, your refusal to give up and your willingness to keep trying different stances will get you there.

And while you're doing all this, concentrating on what you're trying to accomplish and reminding yourself to breathe, the people next to you will be holding poses beautifully. You'll curse them under your breath and wonder why you can't bend the way they do. And then you'll hear the voice of your instructor: "Concern yourself only with your unique situation. This is not a competition. Focus on your goals, not on what your neighbor is doing. Breathe. Steady. Breathe."

Yoga is much harder than it looks. So is parenting. For all of these years, you've been poking and prodding your children along. Then they get to high school, and people tell you to back off, to let them fail, and to force them to face the consequences of their decisions. Nothing is easy about that transition. But you have to hang in there, adjust your stance, find the balance and then hold it, the whole time breathing deeply through the effort and the strain. If you can do that, you'll come out stronger.

Where parents seem to struggle the most is in stepping back from the academic role you might have played in the past. Chances are that you served as a second teacher to your kids, reminding them of deadlines, checking their homework, advocating for them, and protecting their interests. That is appropriate for elementary and middle schoolers who are still children with much physical, emotional, and intellectual growing to do. In high school, however, teenagers are feeling their way into adulthood. They have four years before they become legal adults. At that time, everyone they come across will hold them accountable for their actions. Their college professors won't send you their grades; you will have to count on your children and trust them to tell you how they are doing. Their bosses won't send home progress reports, and you won't have any say-so as to whether your kids keep their jobs. They will be able to get married, join the army, or do whatever they want to do, and you will have little to no recourse. I'm not trying to terrify you. I'm just pointing out that there must be a transitional period in which kids assume greater responsibility for their lives, and that time is now.

What Kids Don't Want

In chapter 4, you met Jeffrey, the King of Excuses. You remember him as a kid whose primary goal was to escape responsibility for his actions, avoid work, and blame others. I'll assume that none of you wants this for your children. You want them to grow into young adults with a strong work ethic, sense of responsibility, and maturity. So it stands to reason that you'd want to hear from kids who are on their way to becoming those kinds of adults. Here's what they have to say about parental involvement in their school lives.

It's totally embarrassing when my parents do my work for me.

"Adam, can I talk to you after class?" I was handing out papers the students had written the week before, and most of the students were eager to see their grades. Adam didn't show the enthusiasm he usually did, and I had my suspicions as to why.

"Yes," he said timidly.

He knows, I thought to myself. *This should be an interesting conversation.*

After class, Adam approached me with hesitation. He kept his focus on the floor, occasionally glancing up at me. I gently broached the subject. "Adam, I didn't hand your paper back with everyone else's because I wanted to talk to you first."

He nodded knowingly but was unable to say what I was thinking.

"I noticed that your paper doesn't sound anything like you. It doesn't seem to be your normal style or voice. Why is that?"

Adam responded with resignation. "My dad basically wrote it."

"Why?" I asked. "You're a good writer; why would you feel that you needed to have a parent do this for you?"

"I didn't," he replied, this time with a spark of anger. "I waited until the night before it was due to write it, and my dad asked me why I was up so late. I told him I had this paper due, and he picked it up and started reading it. He said it was a piece of crap and there was no way I could turn something like that in. Then he sat down and started scratching everything out and basically rewriting everything. It was late and I was tired, so I just let him do it."

The longer Adam talked, the angrier he became. It was obvious that he resented his dad's intrusion. He knew that the work was his responsibility, not his dad's. He hated that he wasn't permitted to turn in his own work, even if it wasn't up to par. Embarrassed that his teacher had identified it and called him out on it, his parting words said it all.

"He treats me like I'm a little kid who still needs his Daddy to help him with his homework. It's ridiculous. I don't know how long he's going to keep doing this, but it's really pissing me off."

Adam apologized to me and vowed to do anything and everything to make sure his dad didn't see his work again. Of course, that was not my wish, but I could understand his frustration and resentment. I also knew that his dad would be heartbroken to hear how his actions had affected his son. Adam had closed the door to any future help from his dad.

I'm afraid that my parents will change my work.

It doesn't matter who you are, how many degrees you have, or how much you want to help your kids with their work. To them, you are just Mom and Dad. You may be an engineer who could put together a killer science project for your kid. You might be an artist who could draw a beautiful portrait for your daughter's art assignment. In my case, I was an English teacher and a writer who could have edited her children's papers. But they wouldn't let me.

My kids never let me so much as look at any paper they ever wrote in high school. I remember thinking that there must be something wrong with them. Why in the world wouldn't they take advantage of me and let me correct their errors so they could earn an A?

"Let me be a resource to you!" I would plead.

"No!" they'd each assert with great conviction. "This is my paper, not yours."

"Yes, but why won't you let me help you? It's always good to have a second set of eyes look at anything you write."

"We're peer editing in class," was the response. "It will be fine, Mom."

Later, after the paper had been turned in and there was no turning back, I'd ask my daughter, the more communicative of the two, what the real deal was. She explained:

"Mom, I love you, but when I have an assignment, I work hard on it. I don't want you to change it or fix it. That feels like you're judging something that I created and am proud of. Besides, I want to find out what grade I get based only on my work, not anyone else's. How will I ever know what I'm capable of if I count on you to go behind me and fix everything?"

"I understand that, I really do," I'd say. "But it just seems a waste to not take advantage of having an English teacher for a mother."

She chuckled. "Even more reason to keep it to myself. How fair would that be to have an English teacher edit my essay? No one else has that advantage. I'd rather just do it myself and get the grade I get. At least that way I know it's my grade."

Ah, the wisdom of children.

I like to be able to ask my parents for help, but I don't like when they force it on me.

Carlos would never call math his favorite subject. He saw the value in learning math concepts and could see where it applied in his life. But he wasn't a left-brained learner and didn't do well with analytical thinking. He was a talented musician who could hear a piece played one time and duplicate it, picking out the tune on his much-loved guitar.

Math homework kept him from guitar-playing more often than he liked. Sometimes he'd create a reward system for himself that really seemed to work. He promised himself that if he worked math problems for an hour, he'd allow himself a twenty-minute break to play his guitar and relax his mind. He'd return to the math feeling a little more rejuvenated and work through it until it was completed.

His system worked, but sometimes he struggled to understand enough to earn a C. When his accountant dad saw his grades in math, he became concerned and sat down to have a talk with Carlos. Carlos described to me later the conversation that followed.

"Son, what's up with the math grade? Can't you do better?"

"Not really," Carlos answered. "Math is hard for me. It's not that I'm not trying; it's just that my brain really doesn't work like that. And it's not all of the time. Sometimes the problems make perfect sense, and I feel really good about them. Other times, no matter how hard I try, I just can't get it."

Dad, always the problem solver, jumped right in. "Well, I can certainly help with that! My job *is* math! Show me your homework and I'll help you with it."

Carlos furrowed his brow. "Dad, I'm not ready to do my math right now. I need a mental break. I just got home from school."

"Come on. Let's do this! I know I can help."

"Yeah, I'm sure you can," Carlos admitted. "But I want to try to do it myself first. Then, when I'm really stuck on something, I'll ask you."

"So playing your guitar right now is more important than getting help from your dad, huh? I see how it is."

Carlos felt his defenses rise. "That's not it at all."

"Okay then, show me the work you've done in the past so that I can see what you're doing wrong."

"Dad!" Carlos yelled. "Back off! I told you that I'll ask you if I need help. If you're going to *make* me show you my work, I don't want the help."

It drives me crazy that they check every single grade I get.

Chun held the returned assignment in her hands, a look of consternation spreading across her face. She had earned a 78, a rare occurrence for a mostly straight-A student. She raised her hand timidly.

"Dr. D., when are you going to put this grade in the grade book?"

"Oh," I responded, "it's already there. I posted these grades this morning."

Chun's face flushed and she closed her eyes, almost as if she were offering up a silent prayer. I couldn't imagine what she was so upset about. To me, a single 78 on one minor assignment wasn't much to worry about. To Chun, however, it was catastrophic.

After class, I stopped Chun to ask her if she was all right.

She shrugged her shoulders then shook her heard slowly. "My parents know every single grade the second it hits the grade book," she explained. "All day, I can't help but think about the talk we'll have when I get home. It's horrible!"

I sympathized. "Chun, just explain to your parents that this was a very tough concept and you'll grasp it soon. After all, it's only one grade, nothing to get upset about."

It was clear by Chun's forced smile and hesitant nod that her parents and I did not share the same philosophy about grades. She spent the rest of the day dreading going home.

My parents spend too much time at school, and it's embarrassing.

Chris was a popular junior who was well-liked by both his peers and his teachers. He played on the varsity football team, had a girlfriend and a solid group of friends, and was self-assured and confident. He had one sister who had graduated from the same school, and Chris was eager to get out on his own just like his big sis.

His parents, however, were anxious to hold onto him, their last child at home. They came to every Friday night football game, which he appreciated and loved. Unlike the other parents who arrived at kickoff and cheered from the bleachers, however, his parents showed up early for the athletes' spaghetti dinner and chatted it up with the coach. They frequently asked if they could review game-day tapes so they could help their son improve. Based on this practice, they made suggestions to the coach as to their son's placement on the field and his need to see more action in the games. They headed up the booster club and took on most of the roles formerly delegated to other parents. Because of their dedication to the team and the money they raised, they expected the coach to acquiesce to their requests and keep their son on the field.

At school, Chris's parents were equally involved. They double-checked Chris's assignments. They emailed teachers to make recommendations on ideas for more engaging lessons. They volunteered to attend every field trip and were the first to sign up for chaperoning duties at the homecoming dance and prom. Some teachers found them to be a godsend; others avoided their calls and emails. They were viewed as helpful by some, annoying and presumptuous by others.

But what really mattered was how Chris felt about their involvement. When asked, he said, "Don't get me wrong, I love my mom and dad. They are so great to me. I know they will always be there for me, no matter what, and I really appreciate that."

Here he paused to collect his thoughts before going on, guiltily but honestly:

"But sometimes it's just too much. I hate to say this, because I know they mean well, but I just wish they would let me have my space when I'm at school. I mean, they're *always* here, and I can't really be myself when I know my parents are watching every move I make."

And then, after another pause:

"It's humiliating when they try to tell my coaches and teachers what to do. I figure that you all hate that and can't help but hold it against me. And I swear, I have nothing to do with that! I've asked them not to interfere, but they don't get it."

He shook his head. "For the most part, I can put up with them being around, but I really, really hate that part."

Sometimes, my parents don't pay as much attention to me as I'd like.

Alexis was a theater kid who lived and breathed her drama class, rehearsals, and the moment she would find out if she got the lead in the school play. Like many theater kids, she was also a bit of a drama queen offstage. She felt deeply, and all of her emotions were evident in her expressive eyes and animated body language.

One day she showed up to theater class with a pained expression on her face, tears stinging her eyes. She blinked hard, swallowed even harder, and tried to steady her quivering chin. Her teacher, Ms. L., got the class started on the day's exercise and then pulled Alexis aside.

"What's wrong?" she asked. "What's gotten you so upset?"

Alexis tried to laugh, but it came out as a choked sob. "It's my parents. I couldn't wait to tell them that I got the part of Sandy and that my best friend got the part of Danny. I mean, what are the chances? You know how long I've been waiting to get a lead like this."

Ms. L. nodded, confused as to the problem. What parents wouldn't be thrilled that their daughter had earned something that meant so much to her?

"They were really happy for me and gave me a big hug. I gave them the show schedule you printed out, and they checked it against their calendars. My parents are really busy, and they were only able to find one night when they could both come." Alexis's voice began to shake. "One night! I thought they'd at least come to opening and closing!"

Ms. L. smiled, everything clear now given Alexis's sensitivity. She suggested that Alexis call her grandparents and share the big news, then invite them to opening night. Alexis brightened some at that idea, but Ms. L. knew that to Alexis, no one replaced her parents.

What Kids Really Want

It's no wonder that parents are confused about the roles they should play in their children's education and activities. Not only do kids vary in their desire for parental input, but a single teenager can change his mind many times about how much time he wishes to spend with his parents. Teenagers will contradict themselves and struggle constantly with finding the balance, just as you do. They want you there, but they don't. And the perfect solution won't be the same from family to family or even from one child to another in the same family.

This means you really shouldn't spend time watching other parents to see what they do. As my yoga instructor would say, "Eyes on your own mat!" Spend your time, instead, watching and listening to your teenagers very carefully. They will let you know how much involvement they want from you and when. This is one of those areas where you should let them call the shots (assuming there are no major areas of concern) and be as flexible as possible. You want them to want you there.

In one example, Chris loved his parents' attendance at football games and the occasional function. But there was a point when his parents crossed the line between supporting him and intruding in every aspect of his life. They needed to stop and ask him how he felt about their attendance at events. Their leadership in the booster club was much appreciated, but it was important for them to provide opportunities for other parents to be a part of their children's lives, too. And they needed to remind themselves that the other adults in Chris's life, namely his coaches and teachers, had their own style of leadership and their own reasons for decisions regarding Chris. Accepting and respecting those relationships would go a long way in letting Chris grow up and discover role models outside of his parents.

Alexis, on the opposite end of the spectrum, sought more participation from her parents. To her, their level of involvement reflected their love for her; to Alexis, lack of attendance at her shows meant lack of interest in her life. Luckily, her parents could take several paths to both assure her and start pushing her out of the nest a bit. If they were in a position to attend more shows, all they would have to do is ask: "Honey, we know you have eight shows. What do you think is a reasonable number for us to attend, keeping in mind that we have other responsibilities?" If they were able to attend only one show, they could couch that with a statement like, "Oh, we hate that we can't come to more of your performances. We'd do anything to be there! We know that Grandma [insert any family member or friend here] wouldn't want to miss this. Let's try to set something up so that everyone goes on a different night. That way, you'll have someone there most of the time." Or, if they were Alexis's only fan club members and extended family lived far away, they would just have to state the reality: "We are so sorry we can't make it. We know it's not the same, but can we get a copy of the video? We can make a night of it—we'll pop popcorn and watch your performance together. That would make us so happy."

The key is to know your children and respect their wishes while being honest with them about your ability to meet their expectations. Remind yourself that in a few years, your children may be a thousand miles away and will need to be able to find happiness on their own. They will need to take care of themselves, advocate for their own best interests, and find joy in other relationships. You are doing the most loving thing possible by nudging them away from you and letting them have their own lives.

The one area where this advice especially holds true is academics. Remember Carlos and Adam and their frustration with their parents' interference? I wasn't making that up. Those are statements I've heard from students time and time again. The consensus among teenagers is that if they don't ask you for help, they don't want your help. Period. They may change their minds if their grades slide or they start to get worried, and when that happens, you should be gracious and offer them some guidance. But if they never solicit help from you in high school, there is a likely explanation.

Teenagers want to know that you believe in them and respect them. They want you to have confidence in their ability to solve problems and meet their responsibilities. Have they earned that? Probably not. But treating them like they are children and expecting the worst from them may very well become a self-fulfilling prophecy. If you treat them like they are incompetent, they will indeed be incompetent. If you tell them they should be ashamed to hand in that paper or project, they probably will be. And they will never, ever ask your opinion on their work again. If, however, you display complete confidence in them, most kids will work hard not to disappoint you. Whether you believe it in your heart is beside the point. Always project the idea that you have confidence in their abilities.

Avoid the Dark Side of Parenting

Please, whatever you do, do not commit the cardinal sin of parenting: doing homework for kids. I would call that the worst of the worst offenses. There is so much wrong with that offense that I hardly know where to start. Everyone—and I mean everyone— is hurt by your decision to do your kids' homework. The messages this decision sends are frightening:

- You tell your children they are incapable of doing grade-level work they should be perfectly capable of doing. In other words, they are not smart enough.

- You tell your children's teachers they are idiots who can't tell the difference between a ninth-grader's project and a sophisticated parent-completed project.

- You tell everyone at the school you have no respect for what they are trying to do. The teacher who assigned that project is planning to get valuable information from it, including whether your children understood the concepts and whether the class can move forward. Now the assignment is worthless to her as an indicator of student understanding.

- You teach your children it's okay to cheat and lie if it means they'll get a better grade in the end.

- Even if your intentions were pure and you just wanted to help, you crossed the line from helping to doing. If your children's final product more closely resembles your work than theirs, you've essentially done their homework for them. You've stolen your children's accountability, sense of self, and sense of responsibility to others, and no matter how you slice it, it comes out wrong.

Another sign that you've crossed over to the dark side of parenting is when you become consumed with every little grade your children earn, like Chun's parents. Here we see where technology can be a fantastic advancement when used properly, a menace when abused. Online grade-reporting programs allow parents to monitor their kids' grades and track their progress in school without having to contact teachers to access this information. But they can be horribly abused.

You're probably not aware of this, but many online grading systems allow teachers to see how many times parents have checked grades. This information is helpful if we've been unable to contact a parent and want to know if the parent is aware of the grades. We check the spreadsheet, see that parents have recently used their login to visit the grade book, and feel a little better. Nevertheless, we are genuinely flabbergasted to see that Chun's parents have checked her grades an average of fourteen times a day. This is not hypothetical—it actually happens. Fourteen times a day. In what sense is this healthy or helpful?

Other parents have an email alert sent every time a grade is entered. Teachers recognize these parents instantly because one minute after we post grades, we get an email or phone call from them. It usually goes something like this: "I just saw Ben's grade on the Spanish quiz he took this morning. Obviously, I haven't had a chance to ask him about it yet, but I will as soon as he gets home. In the meantime, can you tell me what he did wrong?" The kid hasn't even made it through the school day, and his parents are already delving into why he got the grade he did on a ten-point quiz that will probably constitute one-thirtieth of his overall grade. Sometimes I just want to channel the famous blond physical trainer Susan Powter, who used to scream, "Stop the insanity!"

Put yourself in your children's place for a minute. Imagine how you would feel if you were on the receiving end of this kind of intense parental scrutiny. How would you have liked it if you had to explain every mistake or be judged for every step you took? I would have died if my parents had seen some of the grades I earned in high school. Fortunately, I'd see a D on a quiz and know I'd have to do something fast before report cards came out. I'd take ownership of my learning and work my butt off so that when my grades were finally available to my parents, they'd more closely reflect what I could really do. Any teachers worth their salt will tell you that a single grade is almost never indicative of a child's ability. This is why we build in multiple formative and summative assessments that, over time, paint a much clearer picture of what students really know.

I cannot stress enough your need to understand this. Let your kids do their own work, let them stumble, and let them figure out how to do better. If you deprive them of this, or make them miserable by micromanaging their every step, you will do more damage than you will ever know.

Healthy Support

Now, there are times when you *should* involve yourself in your children's work, even when they don't want you to. If you see a pattern of grades or a progress report that indicates your children are not remotely performing to their abilities, you should talk to your children and listen to what they have to say. Share your conversation with teachers and get their input from the classroom perspective. If grade swings stem from social distractions or pure laziness, by all means institute consequences at home and restore privileges as grades improve. If they are academic, schedule a conference and help to formulate a plan. But always place your children in the most active role of the plan. Do not create a situation in which everyone else is working harder than the children themselves. What's important is that you recognize changes in your children's performance and *facilitate* an action plan, without *becoming* the plan.

Let's look at some healthy, supportive actions you can take as a parent. This will help you slowly relinquish responsibility to your growing children while still staying involved in their learning.

Healthy support includes:

- Showing an interest in their lives by asking questions, listening, and following up on previous discussions. Kids will distinguish between casual interest and "creepiness"—aim for the former.

- Attending academic events, games, theater performances—whatever your children are involved in and welcome you to attend. If your attendance makes them nervous and affects their playing, and they are able to admit that to you, don't go. And don't make them feel guilty for being honest with you.

- Sending your kids to camps that extend practice or learning, or grow a love for their chosen activity. Rather than taking over their activities at school, provide them with opportunities to extend their growth outside of school.

- Providing or helping them find resources to be successful, whether they are supplies, a computer, books, or a trip to a library.

- Modeling good organizational and study habits. If they see what these look like in your daily interactions they are much more likely to mimic positive behaviors.

- Stressing the importance of education and actually living it. Show your kids that learning is continuous by taking classes yourself and broadening your own horizons. Remember that they care much more about what you do than about what you say.

- Helping kids think through options: how to complete problems, how to make schoolwork a priority, how to get it all done. Encourage them to take the time to really think and consider various possibilities and roads to success.

- Chaperoning field trips and dances, but only after asking your kids if they are okay with it.

- Asking them if they want you to check their papers or quiz them before their tests. Make the offer and then accept the answer.

- Hosting study groups at your house. You provide the soda and snacks, and they provide the books and brains.

- Creating incentives and consequences at home to correspond with school performance. You have the power to enforce what is happening at school. Celebrate successes and create consequences for poor decisions. Limit TV or Internet time as needed. Take away a cell phone or other coveted item if it's distracting your children from studying for tests.

- Providing opportunities for real-life problem solving and exploration of topics covered in school. You get the fun part: take them to zoos, museums, and botanical gardens to see the real-life application of the textbook learning.

Unhealthy overinvolvement includes:

- Asking teachers to post homework assignments online or send them home so you can remind your kids of all their work. Sure, it's nice to be in the know, and if teachers willingly post this information it's a bonus for you. But kids have to take responsibility for writing down assignments and deadlines without counting on you to remind them. When you are privy to this information, use it for your own decision making (*He can't go out tonight because I know he has a test tomorrow*), but don't use it to take the responsibility away from your children.

- Doing homework, papers, or projects for kids.

- Telling other adults how to do their jobs. Thinking you could teach it or coach it better is one thing; saying it out loud is quite another.

- Reminding kids daily of the places they need to be, including practices, meetings, and jobs. They will never learn to keep a calendar or write a to-do list if you already serve as their constant reminder.

- Calling teachers for clarification on assignments. If your children didn't listen, they should be the ones to approach the teacher for clarification or to come up with an alternate way to get the information they need. Doing this for them just enables them.

- Living vicariously through your kids. This includes forcing kids to pursue your interests, or seeing their successes or failures as your own.

- Asking for extensions, exceptions, or complete forgiveness when kids don't do their jobs. Again, they have to deal with the consequences. If you shield them now, they'll just pay later, and in a much bigger way.

- Insisting on checking all their work before they turn it in.

- Checking their notebooks and otherwise micromanaging their everyday lives. Give them space to discover methods that work for them. Their note-taking systems might look like scribbles to you, but they likely make perfect sense to them.

- Placing focus on grades rather than learning.

Your Involvement on Social Media

Facebook and other modes of social media have become extracurriculars for most kids, and I would be remiss if I didn't discuss your involvement in social media. I'm not going to mince words on this one. The fact of the matter is that if your children have social media accounts, you should have access to them. What kids post can impact every area of their lives, including academics; access to clubs, organizations, and honor societies; and job opportunities. Kids bully online, "date" online, cheat and share homework online, and form and break friendships online. If you ignore this all-important medium of teen social life, you are negligent in your responsibilities. I know that sounds harsh, but it's the truth.

On Facebook, for example, I suggest that you send "friend" requests to your children and strongly urge them to accept them. If they do, your job is then to be silent. Don't say a word on Facebook. Don't publicly comment on their posts or on pictures or on status updates. Before long, your kids will likely forget that you're one of their one thousand friends, and they will forget that you're watching. That is when you will begin to see a side of your children that you probably haven't seen before. Now, when the time comes that they post something wholly inappropriate—and the odds are they will—you must speak to them privately about the image they are conveying. Choose your battles wisely. You might ignore some questionable language but have a serious sit-down about a reference to underage drinking or drug use. You may let a discussion go that you don't particularly like but isn't harmful, but insist that your daughter remove a picture of herself in a seductive pose.

Facebook (not to mention all the other forms of social media) is not going away anytime soon, so you have to view it as a learning tool. It is an excellent venue with which to explore public image and making decisions that will manifest themselves for years to come. I would never tell kids that they can't use Facebook, because it is an indisputably powerful tool in their lives, but for that same reason it must be monitored. It's not an invasion of privacy for you to "stalk their Facebook page" because there is nothing private about Facebook. This will be one of the best lessons your kids will ever learn.

If your kids refuse to "friend" you on Facebook, you have a couple of choices. You can force them to do so or tell them they must discontinue their account. Be aware that when you do this, they will likely open a second account and tell all their friends to use that page instead, so your insistence will get you nowhere. That's why I generally do not recommend this choice. Your second option is to get a friend or family member to "friend" your children and ask that person to alert you to anything of concern. I've done this for friends, and it has worked beautifully. When they must address something worrisome that their kids have posted on Facebook, they don't reveal that I am the source of their information. They simply say, "It's out there in public, and anyone can find the information if they try." This will intimidate kids and further drive home the message that what they post can be visible to all, regardless of the security measures they think they have in place.

It is crucial that you handle your role as Facebook friend to your children with finesse. Monitor, watch, and listen, but stay out of the conversations. Find ways to teach lessons about appropriate online behavior without necessarily calling them out on their specific behavior. And whatever you do, do not post pictures of your teenagers or tell stories about them without getting their permission first. Nothing will get you "defriended" faster than posting a "cute" picture of your teenager when he pranced around the house in his sister's frilly dress at age three. Make your Facebook page about you, and show respect for your children as emerging adults who care very much about their image.

Your other responsibility is to be aware of all of the new social media outlets that pop up on a regular basis. I have a hard time keeping up with them, and I work with teenagers every day, so you will need to do your research. Teens can use their phones to upload photos the instant they are taken, to chat, to tweet, and so on. Ask them to show you all the cool gadgets and programs on their phones, and listen carefully. Pay attention to news items and talk shows that discuss popular sites for teens. Do your homework. You cannot allow yourself to live in the dark ages when it comes to the technology that consumes your children's lives.

It's up to you to find the balance in this and all areas of your children's lives. To do this, you must ask your children to be honest with you and then listen to what they say. Guide and make suggestions. Help with one problem and step away. Be flexible, be strong, and adjust accordingly. And always remember to breathe.

CHAPTER 7

The Real Value of Advanced Placement (AP) Courses— and Who Should Take Them

IMAGINE THAT YOUR CHILDREN HAVE JUST COMPLETED eighth grade and are on the verge of attending high school. You attend the new student orientation, excited to hear all about the high school experience. Administrators, counselors, teachers, coaches—they're all there, just waiting to tell you what to expect. After sharing the school mission statement, taking questions about the lunch plan, and collecting locker fees, the counselors and administrators excuse themselves, and the teachers step up to explain the courses available to your children.

Mr. Regular begins: "Hello everyone, I'm Mr. R. and I teach World Literature at the ninth-grade level. In this class, your kids will read selections out of the textbook and then write in the same style as some of the authors we read. They'll write some poetry, too, when we get to that section of the book. We'll work on vocabulary from our ninth-grade list of most important words. We'll also work on grammar, especially punctuation and other common errors kids this age make. The students will take tests that are a combination of multiple choice, matching, and true-false, with some short-answer questions. When they write essays, they'll have an opportunity to outline, draft, revise, peer edit, and create a final, polished draft. The class is broken up into nine-week sections by units, and there will be multiple minor grades and some projects to balance out the unit tests. I want the kids to do well in my class, so extra credit is always available. I hope to see your kids in my class!"

"He sounds nice," you say to your spouse. "It doesn't sound like things have changed much since we went to school. Papers, reading, vocabulary, grammar—I remember it like it was yesterday."

"Yes," your spouse agrees. "I just hope that Suzanne likes it better than I did. Poetry—ugh!"

Next, Ms. Advanced steps up to the mike. "Hello and welcome! I'm Ms. A., the honors ninth-grade English teacher. I know you have a lot of tough decisions to make about courses for your children, so let me try to help you out with that. In Honors 9, we will be writing—a lot. You're probably wondering what a typical paper might look like. Well, last year, the students enjoyed selecting and then analyzing one of the major themes in *To Kill a Mockingbird*, one of several books they read. The students researched other analyses of their chosen theme, then produced an argument that they supported with textual evidence and their research. As we continued to read further selections during the year, our conversation often turned back to this book as we compared and contrasted multiple authors' viewpoints. As a rule, when we read, students produce their own questions and conduct student-to-student discussions about their findings. Mr. R. mentioned grammar. We do some grammar, as it applies to their individual writing, but students are expected to have a strong foundation in this area. Students must show improvement from paper to paper in order to earn higher scores. They are expected to write at a higher level, incorporating advanced vocabulary that is at least one grade level ahead. Tests consist of thought-provoking essay questions that require thorough, original responses written in class. By the end of the year, your children will have questioned, thought deeply, internalized what they have learned, and challenged themselves with difficult concepts and constant improvement."

"Wow!" you exclaim to your spouse. "That one sounds interesting! Do you think it would be too hard for Suzanne? Do you think she could keep up with the other students?"

"I don't know," your spouse says, deep in thought. "I bet all the smart kids take that class, and if she's not as smart as them, it may hurt her grade point average. In regular English she has a shot at an A. On the other hand, I don't want her coasting through high school, either. Tough call."

And there you have it. It's the discussion heard 'round the world: Should we put our children in advanced classes or regular classes? And how many of each? What's better, a B in an advanced class or an A in a regular class?

The problem is further exacerbated by the fact that you will get varying and often conflicting opinions from other parents, teachers, administrators, and college admissions officers. They all think they have the answer, and to be honest, their answers usually coincide with what they chose for their own kids. What I can offer you are the combined testimonies and experiences of thousands of teenagers who have been there and done that, and how they felt about the experience, both during and after.

Let's begin by defining exactly what advanced classes are, because they are not all created equal. Underclassmen typically have a choice of regular core courses (English, social studies, math, and science) or pre-AP and honors courses. Whether your children's school calls underclassmen courses pre-Advanced Placement (pre-AP) or Honors is just a matter of semantics. Both pre-AP and honors are more advanced than regular classes, but not nearly as advanced as AP courses. Students in pre-AP or honors courses will be expected to perform at a higher level and will likely cover more material in a shorter amount of time than in regular courses. These courses are excellent preparation for students who will later enter AP courses.

AP is offered course by course, so students can choose to take advanced courses only in their areas of strength.

Some schools offer the International Baccalaureate (IB) program, which is an advanced program leading to a special IB diploma. A rigorous curriculum and testing program mark IB, which is a liberal arts, college-level exposure to a wide range of studies. IB is like a prix fixe dinner where every course is decided for you; AP is like an a la carte menu in which you can pick and choose your favorite items. Pre-AP or honors courses are also excellent preparation for the IB program.

To muddy the water further, some schools have strict admissions requirements for advanced classes that may include prerequisite honors courses, teacher recommendations, a minimum overall GPA, a minimum grade in previous classes in the subject area, and/or minimum standardized test scores. Other schools may have no requirements; you need only ask to be admitted to advanced courses. Why the wildly divergent entrance requirements? It all comes down to philosophical ideas about what education should be and what courses should be offered to students.

Some school systems feel that these courses should be earned and that students should have to prove their abilities before being accepted. Others feel that if students want to challenge themselves with more difficult courses, more power to them. Of course, realism is important in this decision. No one wants to see students set up to fail, so if a student has little to no chance of being successful at the level required in an advanced class, it's probably counterproductive to encourage that child to go that route. More and more schools are moving in the direction of open admittance—or at least somewhat relaxed standards—so that a larger number of students can take advanced classes. This places an even greater challenge on parents and students to determine what is best for them.

It's a tough decision, and one that can have lasting consequences, so allow me to share what I have discovered after years of teaching all kinds of teenagers in all levels of classes.

Positive Peer Pressure

We've all heard of peer pressure, and most of us think of it as a highly negative and potentially destructive aspect of the teen years. However, peer pressure can also be used for good, and to greater effect than any pressure we adults can apply. It stands to reason that if this age group cares more about what its peers think than anything else, you will want to surround your children with peers who are actually thinking intelligently. If children are looking to their peers to determine how hard they will work in a class, how cool or uncool it is to be smart, whether it's okay to hazard a guess and possibly be wrong, and whether it's really necessary to do homework, then it almost seems a no-brainer to place your children with peers who are hard working and who care about their grades.

I regularly witness children who become entirely different people depending on the friends who are in class with them. Teachers who struggle with particular students often turn to those students' other teachers to determine if they are seeing the same problems. We are often surprised to learn that Susie, who doesn't do an ounce of work in Teacher B's class and frequently cops an attitude with Teacher B, is an absolute angel in Teacher C's class, always doing her work respectfully. Upon further inspection we find that Susie's friends Jacklyn and Kaitlyn are also in Teacher B's class, and neither friend is a particularly conscientious student. Susie, Jacklyn, and Kaitlyn frequently complain that the work is too hard and that they don't get it. They chat through lectures and take a long time getting down to work. However, in Teacher C's class, Susie sits next to Nancy, a studious, diligent friend. There she stays on task, takes the class seriously, and makes good grades. Susie may look the same in both classes, but everything about her demeanor changes as a result of the other people sitting in the room.

We see this same problem, only on a greater scale, in schools with gang populations and unsafe environments. The mentality becomes one of us versus them, the students too cool for school and the teachers trying desperately to maintain order. The teachers are wildly outnumbered, though, as the students laugh and joke their way through classes, not giving the teacher the time of day and encouraging disrespect among the ranks. Entire classes miss out on instruction because the students feed off each other's lack of interest and negativity. If not identified and remedied in short order, these schools become cultures of violence, poor academic standing, and lost children. If this can happen to an entire school, it can certainly happen in a single classroom.

Even great teachers can have this problem with the wrong mix of students. Yes, good teachers will find ways to maintain order, teach the subject matter, and get it across to those who care enough to listen. But everyone is impacted when a group of students decides that a class is a joke. Unfortunately, this is much more likely to happen in a regular classroom than it is in an advanced one. Regular classes are a heterogeneous mix of varying abilities, and public schools take everyone, including kids with behavior problems and kids who have never been raised to value education. Your children may be part of the problem, or they may suffer at the hands of other students who refuse to learn and who impede those around them from learning.

More Challenging Course Load

Advanced courses, with few exceptions, appeal primarily to kids who want to learn. Children who take these courses know what they're getting themselves into and make the conscious choice to take the more difficult classes anyway. Either they are naturally intelligent and seeking a deeper learning experience or they are average students who want to challenge themselves. Sometimes they are kids forced by their parents to take advanced courses. These kids often lack the internal motivation to be as successful as they could, but they look around at their peers, see them working, and generally adopt the same behavior, even if it is only external. So what we end up with is a combination of kids who might be there for different reasons but who contribute to the tone of a more academically rigorous environment. The mixture is somewhat heterogeneous as well, but now the scales have tipped to the side of "Learning is cool" rather than "Who needs this?"

In addition to the positive student influence in advanced classes, these students also benefit from a naturally more challenging course load. As I have reiterated in previous chapters, most children will rise to reasonably high expectations. They will strive to reach whatever bar is set for them, and these classes guarantee a raised bar. Teachers of these courses expect students who take them to be advanced. This means that instructors won't spend time reviewing or teaching fundamentals but will delve right into concepts that are beyond the scope of the typical grade-level content. They also expect that advanced students will participate regularly in class discussion, complete their homework (which is usually extensive and time consuming), and show a true passion for the content. Look at Figure 3 on the next page. When Mr. R. and Ms. A. described their classes, did you notice some differentiating characteristics?

Mr. R.	Ms. A.
The textbook dictates the instruction in Mr. R.'s class. Designed to correspond with state standards, the textbook drives the curriculum. The mentality is one of getting through the text in order to meet state requirements and pass standardized tests. The content is definitely covered, and the students are learning, but they are following a text rather than their own natural curiosity.	The content dictates the instruction in Ms. A.'s class. While the same (and often more) information must be covered, this class delves more deeply into each unit. Questioning is encouraged. and it's not uncommon to go down unexpected paths, deviating from lesson plans.
In Mr. R.'s class, the assessments are objective, meaning there is one right answer for every question asked. This is apparent when he mentions multiple choice, matching, and true-and-false questions as the basis for his tests. Students quickly learn the right answer, memorize it, and give it back to the teacher as a way to show their knowledge.	In Ms. A.'s class, the assessments are open-ended, meaning students can explore various answers and back them up with examples from their learning. They think critically about their options rather than having answers provided to them. They understand that there can be more than one right answer.
Mr. R. will generally spend however long it takes to review materials, reteach concepts, and retest students until they understand the material.	Ms. A. fully expects her students to understand the concepts relatively quickly. If they do not grasp the ideas during class, they are expected to seek extra help outside of class or do individual tutorials until they catch up with the class.
Mr. R. builds in cushions in his grading to guard against the effects of low test scores. Projects, group work, and extra credit, while valuable, also serve a second purpose of balancing out poor test grades that are meant to indicate student performance.	Ms. A. has no such cushions. Students' grades reflect what they know, and they must demonstrate thorough knowledge to get an A. They don't get a chance to retake a test or get it right the second time. They are expected to learn the information and demonstrate it when asked.

FIGURE 3: *A comparison of class structures, expectations, and pacing between regular and advanced courses*

Before the regular education teachers rise up to defend themselves and regular classes in general, let me make myself perfectly clear: Teachers are as varied as students. Some regular teachers teach exactly like Ms. A., and some advanced teachers never really challenge their students. These descriptions are in no way absolutes. But the comparisons I provide are typical of regular versus advanced classes in any given school. Because regular classes have such a wide range of students, they must build in provisions for the students of lowest ability. Advanced courses don't need to do this. Yes, all good teachers differentiate instruction for varying student strengths, but there is an expectation that students will be well above the minimum standards in advanced classes. In regular classes, we can have a tenth-grade student who has been passed up the grades without demonstrating proficiency and who thinks at the fifth-grade level. Naturally, this will affect how far and how fast teachers can go with classes of thirty students.

So if your children struggle with a subject like algebra, or have trouble remembering large quantities of information in history, or take hours to read a chapter of a novel, their best placement is in a regular classroom. Teachers in these classrooms will differentiate their instruction to meet the needs of several levels of students. They will set a slower pace to cover material and may even provide opportunities for redo's. Essentially, good teachers in average classrooms will do whatever they need to do to meet students where they are and take them to the next level. There is nothing wrong with or inadequate about regular courses following a normal pace. They are appropriate for a large number of students and do what they're supposed to do: teach the content and prepare students for the next year.

AP and honors students are expected to exceed regular standards. Teachers of these courses are less likely to modify assign-

ments or requirements and more likely to hold kids accountable
to deadlines and due dates. They will generally move on if the
majority of the class is ready, and those who are still confused will
have to do extra work outside of school to get to where they need
to be. After all, AP courses are college level, and that's the expectation. Yes, we are still dealing with teenagers, but that doesn't
change the academic requirements of a college-credit class. The
pace is fast and sometimes even frantic. The assessments are difficult enough to challenge these students' college-educated parents. AP is definitely not for the fainthearted.

The Benefits of Advanced Courses

So why push your kids to take advanced courses? Well, the statistics (provided in 2009 by the College Board, developer of the
Advanced Placement Program) speak for themselves:

- The four-year college graduation rate is 62 percent
  higher for students who took an AP English course in
  high school.
- Eighty-five percent of selective colleges say that AP
  courses on high school transcripts favorably impact
  admission.
- Thirty-one percent of scholarship committees consider
  AP classes when determining scholarship recipients.
  That means that nearly one-third of scholarship opportunities will be lost to students taking regular courses
  only.
- More than 3,200 universities accept AP credit. This
  means that if your children pass their exams with the
  scores required by their choice university, they earn
  credit for the equivalent college course, saving substantial dollars in tuition. And your kids are free to explore

more advanced college courses or electives that they might never have gotten the chance to experience.

- Parents can save $8,000 to $19,000 (in-state and out-of-state averages) when students complete their degrees in four years instead of five. AP courses make this more likely.

Aside from these benefits, AP courses offer other positive results. These bonuses reflect the important life skills I encourage throughout this book and foster a love of learning that is priceless:

- Students regularly engage in critical thinking.
- Children explore challenging concepts with other students who enjoy the subject, learning almost as much from them as they do from their teachers.
- Students develop a stronger work ethic. They get a taste of college-level work and learn how to get it all done while still living in the comforts of home.
- Children learn how to study and work for college success. Once they get to college, these students are more prepared and enjoy greater success than those who took regular classes in high school.

So how do you and your children choose what, if any, advanced courses to take? And when are your children taking too many? In chapter 5 we discussed the importance of knowing your individual child and not comparing yourself to other families. It is oh-so-tempting to push children into advanced classes when all of your friends are talking about their kids' AP exams and honors schedules. It is a badge of honor to have children enrolled and doing well in advanced course work, and parents wear it proudly. But kids who don't belong in these courses know it going in or quickly figure it out when information that everyone else seems to understand makes no sense to them whatsoever. Once they discover this and manage to switch their schedules, they are behind in their regular classes and off to an ego-deflating start to the school year. This doesn't mean that your children shouldn't explore advanced options—it just means that they should be selective when doing so.

The beauty of advanced courses is that large schools tend to offer a plethora of choices to cover every interest area and strength. Your child is no math whiz but can get lost in a book of poetry? Sign up for AP Literature. Both of your kids adopted their dad's love of history? Have them take any or all of a series of AP history courses offered nearly every year of high school, all college level, all with the potential to earn college credit. Art, music, every area of science and math—all may be available to your children. Assuming that your kids are strong in at least one area of academics or the arts, they should find at least one or two advanced courses that interest them and push them beyond the regular curriculum. Encourage them in these areas. Challenge them to challenge themselves. Not only will it look good on their transcripts, but it will expose them to a deeper study of their interests and surround them with like-minded students who are potential friends and accountability partners. Let positive peer pressure rear its beautiful head and turn your children's interests into passions.

I could skirt around this next point and be politically correct, but I won't. There are kids out there who are smart. Period. They can take a full course load of advanced classes that cover every subject area and excel in all of them, ending up with a 5.0 grade point average that will get them into Harvard University. And they should! If they can handle that kind of workload without biting their fingernails to the quick, giving up their social lives, and making themselves miserable, then by all means encourage them to have at it. I've had students with photographic memories, and others who listened, never took a note, and got As on even the toughest exams. I've had students whose minds were almost scary, who could analyze, synthesize, and every other "ize" word, while the rest of us were still on step one. There are some truly brilliant young people out there, and they can handle a full schedule of advanced classes. They are somewhat rare, however, so be careful. Kids with five AP courses a day also have hours of homework for each of those courses every night. Is it healthy for seventeen-year-olds to spend twelve to fourteen hours a day on academics? In previous chapters I talked about the importance of sports, activities of interest, downtime, and balance. Can they get any of this with this kind of academic weight?

So again, balance is key. Talk to your children and consider the following questions before deciding on courses:

- What are your children's strengths and interests? They should pursue advanced classes in those areas as much as possible.

- What do the teachers say? Your children might love animals but not have the aptitude or interest to study everything encompassed in AP biology. Teachers can educate you on the expectations for each class and on whether your children are ready to meet those challenges.

- What do their grades reveal? I've had very smart kids who were willing to do only very little work. Grades on previous classes in the subject area reveal much about the effort your children are willing to expend. Little effort in an advanced class often leads to Cs or all-out failure, despite children's level of intelligence.

- What do your children say? Do they want to take advanced courses? If your children have slacked off in the past but now realize the error of their ways, give them a chance to prove themselves. I rarely turn down students who are genuinely contrite about their past mistakes and now want to turn over a new leaf. If you hear, "I know what I did wrong in the past, and I know what I have to do now. I'm willing to work hard in this class. I know I can do it!" it's a good sign that your children are maturing and want to make good on their educational opportunities. Let them.

- Is it time to push them out of their comfort zones? Don't let your kids coast through high school. There is something they are good at, and now is the time to explore that area of interest and strength. Strongly encourage them to take at least one advanced course in high school. Try to do this early on, freshman year if possible, to set a positive tone for academia and show them they are smarter than they think. Doing well in an underclassmen honors class gives them confidence to take a college-level class as a junior or senior. It also has the equally important benefit of exposing them, right out of the gate, to kids who care about learning, kids who will hopefully become friends. Once they've established friends in advanced classes, they will work as hard as they need to to stay there. If they don't have this experience and don't form friendships with kids in these classes, the older they get the harder it will be to push them into advanced classes. So do it early, and if they are successful in those courses, continue to push. This is one area in which you should exert great influence and do everything you can to convince them that they're better off taking the challenge. If they can handle the workload of these courses, do well, and still have a life outside of school, they should continue on this path, whether they really want to or not.

Speaking of doing well, you might be wondering what that means. If your children can earn a B or higher in advanced courses, they are properly placed. A C doesn't look good, no matter how you slice it, but a B in an AP course says something. It says your children might not be geniuses to whom everything comes easy, but they are hard workers who made the decision to challenge themselves when most of their peers chose to take the easier course. Never give your children a hard time for a B in advanced courses, unless yours is one I spoke of earlier who you know for a fact could have earned an A. These courses are difficult—they have to be or they wouldn't be college level. Keep that in mind, always. Expect to see lower grades, especially initially, until your children get a handle on the expectations. Look for improvement and engagement as the semester progresses. But try not to harp on grades. You are hoping that your children will come out of these classes as critical thinkers with strong work ethics and a desire to pursue their passions. Keep your focus on the big picture.

And remember that sometimes these courses are exactly what children need to gain some confidence in their abilities. I'll end with a story that demonstrates how that can happen.

CASE IN POINT

Emma came into high school believing she was average. She had made average grades in middle school, had been tested and denied entry into the gifted and talented program, and was surrounded, it seemed, by kids who were smarter than she.

She requested a front-and-center seat in my freshman honors class. She smiled and nodded as I taught, wrote down everything that was said, and listened intently as her peers contributed to the conversations. She asked questions that let me know she wasn't on the top academically, but she passionately wanted to be.

When I passed back the results from the students' first assessment, her face said it all. She fought tears, nervously glancing around at others' grades for comparison. After class, she came to me and asked what she could do to improve. "I'm better than this," she said, through a tight throat. "I love this class and I understand everything we cover. I just don't test well. But I know I can do better if you give me a chance."

"Emma," I replied, "I'm not the one who has to give you a chance. You are. You are new to this class, and high school is a whole different ballgame from middle school. I know you can do this, too. I have full confidence in you. You just need to give yourself time to adjust, read my comments on your test, apply what I've told you, and keep working hard."

Emma nodded her head, relief slowly creeping over her face. "Thank you," she said simply, and walked out.

As the semester progressed, Emma had good days and bad. She conquered some of her demons, improved gradually in other areas, and continued to struggle with a couple of concepts. The other students were constant and unintentional sources of encouragement. They didn't realize it, but their interest and engagement and love for learning fueled Emma's interest. She was thrilled to be surrounded by kids who cared, who weren't afraid to be smart and to admit that they liked learning. She began to study with them, adopt some of their learning techniques, and raise her hand even when she wasn't sure of the answer.

Peer influence, the atmosphere of the classroom, and high expectations emboldened her to think on a more sophisticated level and to work in a more efficient manner. She didn't become brilliant overnight or months later outshine her peers. But she gradually improved and adopted study habits that would serve her well for years to come.

Near the end of the semester, Emma approached my desk once more and spoke confidently to me. "I have to say something to you, because you really need to know this."

"Okaaaayyy," I said cautiously, wondering what was coming next.

She smiled. "Nah, it's all good," she began. "You don't know this, but last year I told my parents I wanted to take honors in high school, and they didn't think I could do it. They knew I wanted it, but they weren't sure if I could handle the difficulty.

"They went to my teachers and counselors and asked them what they thought. They were all in agreement that I couldn't handle the workload. I wasn't gifted and talented, like all of my friends, so I couldn't take the advanced classes in middle school."

Here Emma stopped and collected herself. The memory clearly affected her. She thrust her shoulders back and smiled. "I told them they were all wrong. I told them I could do it. No one believed in me, but I believed in myself. And I just want to thank you for being the one person who told me I could do this and for meaning it."

It was one of those teacher moments you read about in forwarded emails and Facebook links that are shared 5,324 times. Some find it corny or cheesy, but it happened, and it was 100 percent real for this student and for me.

"Emma, that is so sweet, but you are giving me too much credit," I said. "You're here and you're successful because you made the decision to be. I'm so proud of you for proving everyone wrong in the best way possible."

We shared a hug and a smile, and she went on to her next class. Emma was the perfect example of someone who didn't fit the mold of the advanced student but who wanted it and made it happen. Sometimes all the experts are wrong.

So it seems that smart doesn't guarantee success, and average doesn't relegate a person to mediocrity. Work with your children to assess their strengths and weaknesses, encourage them to challenge themselves, and send them the message that ultimately it is up to them to get the most out of whatever classes they choose.

CHAPTER 8

College Isn't for Everyone: Is It Best for *Your* Child?

F ROM ONE EXTREME TO THE OTHER, OR SO IT MAY SEEM. In chapter 7, I talked about encouraging your children to take at least one advanced course and challenging them to pursue their interests and strengths at a higher level. The title of this chapter might seem contradictory to this advice, but it is not.

Your children's interests may have little to do with academics, and their strengths may manifest themselves in a wide range of modalities that have nothing to do with studying a certain way or passing myriad tests to prove one's intelligence. That's okay. Despite what the American educational system tells you, not every child can or should go to college.

Remember when you were in high school and got the opportunity each day to take at least one class that wasn't academic? You'd hurry to Shop to set up whatever project you were working on. Donning gloves and goggles, you'd delight in fifty minutes of power equipment and sawdust. You'd fix things and build things, carting your creations around school as if they didn't matter, when in fact, they really did. You were proud of your ability to use your hands in practical, beneficial ways. It is a skill you've used throughout your life, and to this day, you still love tinkering in the garage, fixing the seemingly unfixable.

You can also change your own oil and determine why your engine won't start, thanks to all those hours spent in the high school garage working on teachers' cars. You've saved thousands of dollars on mechanics by knowing how to properly maintain your automobile. Your sister still sews her curtains for her home and Halloween costumes for her kids every year. She took Home Economics in high school, and while some thought it a waste of time, she's enjoyed years of sewing for her family and has saved a lot of money in the process.

Maybe your cousin is a hairstylist. She reserves her own space, works her own hours, and charges $150 for a cut and color, which takes approximately an hour and a half. She's married to a plumber who is in constant demand, charges double time on weekends, and makes enough money for the family to live comfortably and even take the occasional vacation. Your nephew, who always hated school, just landed a role in an off-Broadway play. He is scraping by in New York, sharing an overpriced apartment with four other people, eating Ramen Noodles, and he is happier than he's ever been in his life.

Your neighbor, who lives in a similar house to your own, never went to college but put herself through respiratory therapy training. After two years and the granting of her certification, she makes good money working 9 to 5 on the weekdays. She has excellent medical benefits through a network of doctors located right at the facility where she works.

If you think about it, I'll bet you can name a substantial number of people in your life who never went to college, or who did but never used their degrees, and who are now providing for their families and living happy lives. Yet we continue to perpetuate the myth that only college graduates are successful. Doing anything different is "a waste," according to the prevailing sentiment. Yes, most college grads make more money in the long run while enjoying the perks of white-collar professions, but that doesn't mean there are not plenty of alternatives available to our new generation of workers.

The idea that everyone should go to college came about when schools took a misguided approach to eliminate tracking. Tracking lost favor because it implied that students were "tracked," much like a train unable to change courses. Some students were sent down a path toward office work, homemaking, or woodworking, while others were guided toward classes that would prepare them for college. Members of the educational community, parents, and politicians feared that tracking was inequitable, even elitist, and began to view vocational programs negatively. But before we got the idea that vocational programs were somehow lesser than their academic counterparts, vocational schools were popular alternatives to college and did a fine job of preparing kids for life after high school. Once the tracking discussion dominated educational circles, society took on a condescending attitude toward trade learning and that attitude spread to the companies that funded and donated to the programs. Equipment eventually became outdated, and the classes were viewed as dumping grounds for kids who "couldn't hack it" in regular classes. In other words, when we lost respect for noncollege alternatives, we also lost the funding and high-level standards that had fortified the programs. And it was all because it looked good to make the broad, generalized statement that everyone could go to college. Everyone was smart enough, everyone was able. Everyone, regardless of hardship or intellectual ability or internal motivation or level of interest, could and should go to college.

The response? Think about it. We had kids who chose vocational programs because that was where their interest lay. We had kids who knew they'd never go to college but found hope in opportunities that would be at their doorstep if they just graduated high school. We had kids who didn't process like other kids did, who didn't grasp school learning but who had street smarts and common sense. We had kids who were pregnant, or who didn't have money for college, or who simply had no idea what they wanted to do with the rest of their lives. And what became of all those kids? Well, they dropped out. And they continue to drop out. Some try college—as the only option offered to them—and of those few, many quickly flunk out.

So our political posturing and insistence that every kid could succeed and that meant every kid could go to college actually took away options and caused kids to give up. We in academia know and understand the importance of choice in all we do. Every educational leader out there espouses choice in classroom activities, teaching to various learning styles, providing opportunities for kinesthetic learners, giving creative kids a chance to express themselves, being aware of auditory and visual learners, and on and on and on.

And then we tell all teenagers that they have to go to college or they are failures.

This presumption not only hurts kids, but it also cripples society. Currently, we have students who had no business going to college failing miserably. According to Mike Bowler with *U.S. News & World Report*, roughly 30 percent of all college freshmen in 2009 dropped out in the first year, and 50 percent of those who started college never graduated.[1] Remember when colleges used to cater to the better-than-average student? Well, it should tell you something that over a million students attending community colleges are currently enrolled in remedial classes. In an attempt to retain more students, these colleges spend a fortune, to the tune of $2.5 billion a year, to offer remedial classes to students who cannot pass without extra help.[2] You'd better believe that the colleges aren't going to just absorb that cost. Instead, they raise tuition, which students can't afford, leading them to take out exorbitant loans that they must begin paying off soon after they graduate. When that day comes, only half of them will find jobs in which they actually use their degrees, according to a 2013 report from the U.S. Bureau of Labor Statistics.[3] The other half will take jobs that don't require degrees, or they will live in their parents' homes indefinitely, all the while accruing more debt.

Now, those who graduate with degrees will get higher-paying jobs that help secure their futures. They will do what we hope all college graduates will do and find success in their chosen fields. College remains a desirable choice that helps create a well-rounded, well-educated citizenry, and that is positively crucial. We need college graduates—lots of them. But in order to be successful in college, high school students need to have the intellectual ability, personal motivation and drive, a high school course load that prepares them for postsecondary education, and realistic goals based on strengths and interests. Do all students have these qualities? As a long-time teacher, I can tell you my answer is a definitive *no*.

And I don't consider that to be a problem, necessarily. After all, we live in a world that functions at many different levels, and we need people performing at every one of them. According to a 2011 report by the Harvard Graduate School of Education, "The United States is expected to create 47 million jobs in the 10-year period ending in 2018, but only a third of these jobs will require a bachelor's or higher degree. Almost as many jobs—some 30 percent—will only require an associate's degree or a post-secondary occupational credential."[4] These statistics should be a comfort to children and parents for whom college is not an option. They should be a joy to teenagers who have determined that college is not for them, because they show that young adults do have options, and if they choose to take them, they are not failures.

Bypassing College: A Sampling of True Stories

In my career, I've worked with innumerable kids who I knew wouldn't make good college students. Here's a peek into these extraordinary and not-so extraordinary kids' lives and what you can learn from them. See if you recognize your own children in these examples.

Colin

Colin was smart and capable. He showed signs of intelligence and inquisitiveness from an early age, when he would build intricate skyscrapers out of Legos. When asked as a young child what he wanted to do when he grew up, he'd quickly and excitedly answer, "Be an architect!" But as he grew older, he became less interested in his early passions. His parents' divorce, coupled with their constant push for Colin to be the first in the family to go to college, transformed a strong-willed child into a defiant one. The more his mother encouraged him to prepare for college and use his brain, the more he rebelled. He earned As on tests, but he refused to do any class work, so he frequently failed classes. The ability was there, but the desire and motivation to learn was not. Plenty could have been done at the time to turn this young man around, including therapy, redirected parenting skills, and motivational tools that might have helped him find the drive he had buried, but nothing was done. When it was obvious that he would be lucky to graduate high school and that college was out of the question, his mother reluctantly searched for options. Three years later, she's still looking. Meanwhile, Colin lives at home, occasionally works a fast-food job for a few months or so before getting fired, and has no goals or ambitions. As far as he's concerned, life is what happens to him. He passively waits for something to happen.

Carl

Some kids don't just enter the classroom, they make an entrance, instantly infusing the atmosphere with their energy. Carl was that kid. His laughter was infectious and his face was animated, his arms flailed as he spoke, and if eyes actually could sparkle, his did. He was a theater kid, the kind who loves nothing better than performing before a roomful of people. I remember seeing him for the first time in a musical and recognizing immediately that star quality that eludes most of us. He was a triple threat—an actor, singer, and dancer—and he was phenomenal at all three. Beyond this talent, Carl had total dedication to his dream and an awesome capacity for continually rebounding and refocusing to keep moving forward. When he left high school, college wasn't on his radar, but Broadway was. Naysayers saw it as a pipe dream, something that happens so rarely that it wasn't even worth pursuing. Besides, wouldn't college be more practical?

Carl didn't listen. He graduated, moved to New York, and never looked back. He is now an award-winning Broadway star. I leaf through magazines and see him in all his splendor, reaping the benefits of being a nontraditional student. Success comes in many packages, and his is beautifully wrapped.

Abby

Abby struggled in school, and not in one particular subject but in all of them. She didn't have any learning disabilities; it just took her longer than average to process ideas. She really needed to think to understand what many of us grasp almost immediately. Studying was a tedious process, reading comprehension was slow, and problem solving was extremely difficult. Abby just wasn't a great student, in the traditional sense. Yet she wanted to be a surgeon. She believed she was going to be a surgeon. And her entire family encouraged her into a false sense of hope that she would actually become a surgeon. Let me just say the thing I'm not supposed to say: It was never going to happen. Drive and the will to make things happen can indeed make things happen, but first and foremost, one has to have the ability. Without the ability, all the wanting in the world wouldn't turn Abby into a smart, quick-thinking, deft surgeon.

The problem was that Abby's parents were so concerned about her self-esteem that they were afraid to be realistic with her about her strengths and weaknesses. When Abby graduated and had trouble even getting into a local college, she got her first dose of reality. She looked at her resume, saw her GPA as if for the first time, and felt cheated. She had been lied to for years and led to believe she could do something she couldn't. Having never considered alternative paths for her life, Abby graduated with a sense of hopelessness and with no solid plans for her future.

Greg, Ben, and Natalie W.

The three kids in the W. family all graduated high school with average grades. Not one of them had the slightest desire to go to college. Neither of their parents had gone, and both were doing just fine financially. Greg had taken some vocational courses in high school (his school was one of only a few still offering them), and he found that he was skilled at the finer aspects of building and woodworking. Upon graduation, he sought out and obtained an apprenticeship with a carpentry master. Twenty years later, he has a long, distinguished career as a consummate cabinetry man. He is never without work and supports his family comfortably.

His brother, Ben, graduated high school and immediately entered a respiratory therapy program. He earned his certification after two years and was able to begin his new career with steady pay and excellent health benefits at the age of twenty.

Since then, he has renewed and added multiple certifications, gained invaluable experience that has brought him promotions and raises, and contributed to saving and improving thousands of lives. He loves his job.

Natalie explored several positions but primarily worked as a secretary, attaining business and communication skills and the respect of everyone with whom she worked. After fifteen years of learning the ins and outs of the corporate world, putting away her money, and developing a business plan, she started her own small company. She now works for herself, whatever hours she chooses, and wouldn't have it any other way.

Cameron

Never an appreciator of academics, Cameron loved one subject, history. He lost himself in the stories of wars and soldiers fighting for their country. Perhaps it was because he came from a long line of marines and had been living *Semper Fi* for as long as he could remember. One of the schools in our district offered a Reserve Officers' Training Corps program that interested students from other districts could attend. Cameron asked his parents if they would allow him to switch to that school and they agreed. Soon, Cameron was wearing a uniform, exhausting himself at physical training, learning to shoot a rifle, and studying his favorite subject, history. Cameron fell into pace quickly. He loved the emphasis on duty and honor and grew a special bond with Major Kerry, his instructor. Kerry told entrancing stories of traveling around the world, experiencing unfamiliar cultures, and making lifelong friends during his years of service.

When it came time for Cameron to make plans for after high school, he decided that the Marine Corps was exactly where he needed to be. Kerry had talked to him about his options, and he knew that after giving some time to his country, he could later go to college for free if he wanted to. But Cameron wasn't even thinking that far in advance. All he wanted to do was call himself a United States marine.

Michelle

Michelle was a senior in high school when her parents insisted that she go to college to become a pharmacist. Pharmacy, quite honestly, was the last thing on her mind. She could understand her parents' desire for her to land a secure, respectable job making good money, but her interest lay in cooking, not science. Her parents came from a long line of college grads and saw anything other than university as a waste. They acknowledged Michelle's interest in cooking, but only as a hobby for a well-rounded woman. In their eyes, cooking was a task, not a career. Michelle wanted to please her parents, and since they were footing the bill for tuition, she allowed them to call the shots.

During her first year of college, Michelle failed Chemistry 101. She took the same class second semester and failed again. She didn't like her classes, in general, and didn't love college like all of her friends did. Heading home over the weekends to de-stress, she did what made her happy: she baked. Cooking was her escape, her quiet pleasure. When summer came and her friends traveled and relaxed, Michelle took chemistry a third time, this time finally passing. Her parents encouraged her, "See, you can do it. You just needed to put your mind to it." Having had no summer break, Michelle returned to school for her second year, this time taking slightly more advanced classes. She struggled and escaped to her home as much as possible, and when grades were released at the end of that semester, her worst fears had come to fruition. She had failed two courses this time, one of them the dreaded Chemistry 200. Her parents threw up their hands. Michelle felt like a failure. She began to unravel, depressed, anxious, trapped in a major for which she wasn't suited and in which she had no interest, with nothing but dread for the future.

Eventually, after two more semesters of poor grades and increasing depression, Michelle told her parents what she had told them at age seventeen—that she wanted to go to culinary school and become a chef. Frightened of what might happen if they didn't relent, they agreed to allow her to pursue her dream. After years of tuition paid toward a degree Michelle never wanted, her parents are now paying for culinary school. And Michelle is thriving. She developed a recipe that won recognition and acclaim, her old spirit has returned, and she is finally doing what she was meant to do all along.

What About Your Kids?

Right about now, you're probably wondering where your children fit into all this. If your teens don't necessarily resemble one of the students above, does it mean they should pursue college? Well, it depends. See if you recognize your children in any of these groups of kids who might not or should not be college-bound:

- Kids who aren't "school kids." They flat out tell you they don't like school, they do the bare minimum to squeak by, and they have a hard time sitting still all day.

- Kids who struggle through all or most academic subjects. School drains them because everything is hard for them to comprehend and process. They may excel at noncerebral activities or have skills in other areas, but academia just isn't a strong suit.

- Kids who have no idea why they are going to college, other than it is expected of them. They are seniors and don't have the slightest notion what they want to do with their lives. They've taken no steps to determine majors that might be a good fit or careers that are a strong match. Nor do they have a plan to take liberal arts classes and determine a major after their freshman year. In other words, they've put zero thought or preparation into college.

• Kids who have a passion and a talent for something non-school related. They wish to pursue creative endeavors (music, art, theater), have hearts for service (health care, customer service, the ministry), or prefer hands-on training for skill-based jobs (plumbers, electricians, masonry workers).

• Kids who have no appreciation for the classroom environment but who love to tinker, explore, and create. Look at the entrepreneurs and societal icons we revere who make more money than all of us put together and who never finished college. They are few and far between, but they prove it can be done.

• Kids who have no internal drive to take college seriously or to view it as an expensive investment. These kids talk about nothing but the fun they'll have. They will drain your piggy bank before they flunk out of school. If all they care about is the football team and getting into a fraternity, be worried.

• Kids who are extremely immature or clearly need time to grow up a great deal before living on their own. These kids have options that include community college, working until they acquire some maturity, and living at home while taking a couple of college classes. Sending them off to overnight freedom and the responsibility of a full course load, however, will probably not end well.

Think about the *U.S. News & World Report* statistics I presented earlier. The Harvard Graduate School of Education reported in 2011 a 56 percent average dropout rate among college students.[5] If the "college might not be for us" groups I just described pursued options for which they are better suited, imagine the decline we would see in the dropout rate. Think about the money that is thrown away on tuition for kids who never should have gone to college in the first place. Think about the mounds of debt accumulated by students who never used their college degrees. Young adults have options, and your job as parents is to expose them to their options, remain open-minded yourself about what your kids can do, and support their decisions to pursue their interests. Their dreams for themselves might not be your dreams at all, but you need to respect them anyway.

Now, if your children are interested in college but have reservations, you should allay their fears and encourage them to attend. You will have a good sense of your children's abilities to be successful in college based on your recognition of the following characteristics:

- **They are good students but are tired of school.** Everyone gets tired of school. Taking them to visit colleges and introducing them to all that college has to offer (including the nonacademic opportunities) should reignite the flame of interest. Once they realize that college is a whole new world with opportunities they can't find anywhere else, they'll find their excitement.
- **They want to go to college but claim to need a year off to travel, take a break, or work.** Increasingly, kids are doing this, and I caution against it. I can't tell you how many kids I've taught who have taken a one-year break and have yet to enroll in college five years later. It sounds good on paper and makes sense to adults who have worked all their lives and would kill for a year off, but

don't fall for this arrangement. They can travel, work, and take breaks in the summer. Keep the ball rolling. Get them right into college.

- **They have a few interests but aren't sure what they want to major in or pursue as a career.** This describes most kids, so there's nothing to fear here. For example, Cecilia Capuzzi Simon found that in 2012 at Penn State University, 80 percent of freshmen reported uncertainty about their majors.[6] That's part of what college is for—to explore options through general and liberal arts courses in order to determine an area of interest. Kids who enter college should self-assess and have some idea of majors, but most don't need to make a decision until their junior year.

- **They are still a little immature and needy or fear they aren't ready.** These kids are exactly the ones who need the push, and college will provide that. If they are typical teenagers in that they are eager to be free but anxious about taking care of themselves, college will be good for them. Teach them the basics and then push them out of their comfort zones. They and every other kid around them will figure it all out.

- **They have several interests and only one of them is college.** Those interests can often be fostered in college and converted into much-loved careers. If college can turn a passion into improved job opportunities and marketability, it is the preferred choice. If not, interests can still be retained through college and well into life as hobbies; it's not an either-or proposition.

Keep in mind as you and your children are making this important decision that you have a wealth of information at the high school. Teachers of various subjects, counselors, coaches, and club sponsors are all valuable resources who can give you insight into your kids' talents, abilities, weaknesses, work habits, and levels of motivation. Use these resources! They will fill in the missing gaps of information and can objectively report on your children's readiness for college. They can also confirm or validate your children's talents and help you decide if your kids have what it takes to be successful in college or in the workplace.

What You Can Do Right Now

There are several things you can do at this point to help your children determine their future paths:

- Access the many free career and interest surveys available on the web. These tools help your children do what is often difficult for them: self-assess. Surveys can paint a surprisingly accurate picture, and kids generally enjoy discovering the insights they provide. They may reveal careers your children never knew existed or solidify kids' ideas about what they should do when they graduate.

- Help your children explore careers and try to expose them to possibilities they might never have considered. Introduce them to people in various fields and have them shadow or intern for a day.

- Send the message that there is value in all types of jobs. College is a great option, but it's not the only option.

- Let your children follow their own paths. Try not to project your personal desires onto your children. Just because you love science doesn't mean your children will. Just because you went to college doesn't mean that's the answer for your children. And don't try to get them to be what you couldn't. It's not their job to fulfill your dreams.

- Always place value on education of every kind, including academic, training, advanced degrees, and certifications and licenses. Learning is fantastic, but it shouldn't be limited to the college classroom. The greatest success stories come from people who are lifelong learners, who act as sponges soaking in whatever they can, not just about careers, but about life.

- Do everything in your power to intervene if you see signs of your children feeling defeated and wanting to quit. Colin, the smart high school student who gave up because of a series of personal problems could have been redirected down a more positive path with the right intervention. Counseling, working with teachers, using positive reinforcements, finding inspiring role models— whatever it takes, step in. These are crucial years that call for aggressive interventions.

- Accept your kids for who they are and enjoy every minute of what makes them special. Carl had a special talent, and everyone around him knew it. It would have been a shame if his parents didn't foster that talent but instead expected him to be like every other kid. Keep in mind Michelle and Cameron, whose focus was sincere and impassioned. Unbridled, these kids can go places.

- Be realistic about your children's abilities. Abby was never going to be a surgeon, and she's not alone. Drive can overcome a lot, but it can't be the only tool in the box. Help your children to research college admission requirements and acceptance rates, along with qualifications for careers of interest. Let them see for themselves whether they can cut the mustard. Help them realize that while their first choice might not be doable, they have plenty of other options that are suitable.

Finally, as always, listen to your kids. Not only is it their future, but if they're not invested from the beginning, they likely won't be invested at all. Get them on board early, and guide them in their decisions through the entire process. You are older and wiser and have much to offer them in the way of life planning and goal setting. Share your knowledge, but understand that whatever they choose for their lives, they will have to make it happen. If your kids are on the fence about college, by all means encourage them to go that route. But if they are adamant that college is not for them, believe them.

CHAPTER 9

The Dangers of Coddling: Helping Your Kids Develop Healthy Self-Esteem

THINK BACK A DECADE. IT IS A BALMY SATURDAY AFTER-noon in May. Your young soccer kids have just wrapped up three months of missed goals and consistent offsides, but they have enjoyed a lively season as a close-knit team. The players are meeting for an end-of-season pizza party to celebrate their camaraderie and persistence on the field. Faces covered in sauce and belches hanging in the air, the kids eagerly await the presentation of their trophies, ceremoniously granted to each of them. They lost most of their games and never even entered a tournament, but each gets a trophy because everyone is a winner.

Flash forward to today. Your children's rooms are littered with trophies, but your son never did make the competitive high school soccer team, and your daughter has played on junior varsity for three years, most of that time warming the bench. They both grew up thinking themselves young David Beckhams and Mia Hamms, thanks to the endless recognition and praise they received at every game. You even started to believe it yourself, despite the fact that you paid for those trophies every year: Not one of them was presented by a higher authority recognizing true talent.

This story, and others like it, is so common that we have created a name to represent this generation: the "everyone-gets-a-trophy" children. That name speaks volumes about the kids we have raised and the disservice we have done them. Yet in many ways, we continue that tradition in all areas of kids' lives, from academics to sports to clubs to family responsibilities. Constant praise, endless props, criticisms gently couched in encouragement—it is a wonder we are not all exhausted from the constant need to uplift our kids and protect their self-esteem.

You know what they say about good intentions, right? We thought that by increasing our kids' self-esteem we would also increase their achievement. If they believed in themselves, they could do anything! No one is arguing that believing in oneself and taking pride in one's accomplishments is a bad thing. We need to feel that we are doing well, and it is normal to want to be acknowledged when we do. What took us into dangerous territory, however, was when we started praising kids regardless of whether they were deserving. We wrongly confused positive reinforcement with praise, and while these concepts belong to the same family, they are as different as your children.

Positive reinforcement is acknowledging when children do something well in order to encourage them to keep doing it. I discussed this at length in chapter 1, so you know what I'm talking about. Remember Ashley, who wasn't thrilled about helping with chores, so you used positive reinforcement to inspire her to pitch in, work a little more diligently, and contribute to the household responsibilities? This motivational technique is meant to galvanize children who are at the beginning stages of learning a new task or taking on a new challenge. It is effective, it is appropriate, and it works. Ashley will depend on your feedback initially, but she will discover her own internal spirit and will no longer need outside reinforcement to want to do a good job.

Praising, however, involves nothing short of heaping accolades upon someone. It is commendation, approbation, and acclamation. It is an end result of a job well done or the glorification of a person or act. It is what you extend to your daughter when she finishes her last performance of a two-week theater run, your own personal "Brava!" to her hard work and dedication. It is lauding your son after the painting he submitted to the Arts Council contest won first place and special recognition. It is a blue ribbon, a final grade of an A, a standing ovation.

What it is not, or shouldn't be, is effusiveness at every landmark or milestone, recognition of every act, or a false sense of hope that kids are more talented or smarter than they really are. To many parents, that is what it's become, and it is evident in their children. Abby, from chapter 8, was a prime example of this, a struggling student whose parents had convinced her she could be a surgeon. Anyone who suggested otherwise was met by Abby's shocked indignation and her parents' demands for an apology to repair Abby's wounded ego.

Abby is one of a considerable number of teenagers who fall apart at the slightest criticism and are truly dismayed when they are told they are wrong. I've seen it daily for years and continue to see it. Accommodating this generation became a priority about seven years ago, when, for example, teachers were told to replace their red pens with green ones. Red pens, it seemed, screamed "You're wrong!" and made sensitive students feel that we had "bled all over their papers." Green, on the other hand, was a "friendly, nonthreatening" color. I never switched to green, because, well, the whole idea was stupid. Not only did red make exactly the point I wanted to make, but I drove the message home even more strongly by referring to it as my Red Pen of

Justice. My former students still reference my infamous red pens and were never scarred by my choice of ink.

Teachers are also told to balance negative feedback with positive. This means that every time they grade a stack of papers, they are instructed to dutifully jot down some pleasantries in the midst of honest feedback regarding, for instance, disorganized ideas or inaccurate content. Imagine a math teacher having to write "Good thought process!" on a problem that has been worked incorrectly and resulted in the wrong answer. That's what teachers have been told to do for years now. But some teachers don't listen to that directive. If they have something nice to say, they say it. If they don't, they don't make something up. Instead, they reserve their praise for the truly praiseworthy work, thereby increasing its value. They allow their students to experience the true joy of having received a genuine compliment from teachers who don't fake compliments. Do you do the same? Do your compliments mean something, and do they carry value?

Another directive commonly given to teachers is to avoid telling students they are wrong when they venture a guess in classroom discussion. We are supposed to nod sagely and say we can understand why students would think that, and then gently steer the discussion toward the correct answer, all the while protecting their fragile egos. Now, I teach literature, and often there really are several "right" answers, since so much of literature involves interpretation. So in my class, it is okay to have different opinions about the author's purpose, as long as those opinions can be supported with the text. However, sometimes the meaning is clear, and sometimes students completely miss the meaning. And I try to be honest with my students about this, telling them, "Kids, sometimes you are wrong, and I will tell you when that happens. I always want you to venture a guess, but if you missed the boat, I'll let you know." The first time I do, some kids audibly gasp.

Seriously. They gasp that a teacher would tell a student he is wrong. But it is a teacher's job to teach, and we don't do them any favors by letting them go through life misinformed. The same applies to parents and your responsibility to be honest with your kids when they are getting it wrong. A tactful, "No honey, that's not the way it works," will not leave lasting scars.

Overly Great Expectations

My concern is not so much the kids who are initially surprised by honesty but then cope with it, but those who never learn to accept it because it doesn't jibe with what they have always been told and now believe about themselves. They have been coddled and cushioned and lied to about their abilities their entire lives. Then someone comes along and tells them where they really stand. Don't get me wrong, you should be supportive and share laughter and warmth, and your kids should take comfort in knowing that they can take chances. But you shouldn't lie to your kids to protect them, and some of them want and expect that. What they have is not healthy self-esteem; it is a dangerous form of narcissism that comes from a delusion about their abilities.

These kids expect to be rewarded for everything they do, regardless of how ordinary it might be. In their minds, others should feel privileged to know them and spend time with them. When they get weekend jobs, they are appalled to discover that they are expected to clean bathrooms as part of their duties. They make no pretense about their refusal to do so, since bathroom cleaning is clearly beneath them. They see customers' rudeness as a sign of disrespect and offer little to no respect in return. For these teens, the customer is most definitely not always right. They will not offer to help with anything beyond the scope of what they think they should be doing; there is no spirit of teamwork in order to get a job done. And when their job evaluations come and they are less than glowing, they are furiously insulted and usually quit.

These same kids are completely convinced that they will graduate high school, get into a competitive college, and earn six figures in their first career. Books have been written that address this generation's belief in its superiority. These books exist to help companies understand and cope with this generation, both in interviews and as new hires. Since young adults' self-esteem has been protected for so long, they are unable to handle criticism and life in the real world, and they crumble under the pressure and the honesty. Yet they fully believe they are worth exorbitant salaries and fully expect pay raises within a few months of employment. The fact that companies are trained in how to work with this generation would be funny if it weren't so sad. Even the "real world" attempts to accommodate these kids' narcissism.

One of the scarier notions about kids in this group is that they believe effort—regardless of results—should be rewarded. Frequently when I hand back an assignment, at least one student stays after class to tell me his grade is unfair because he tried. "I worked really hard on this, so I deserve an A," has become the mainstay philosophy in teenagers' brains. I can't help but trace this mentality back to all of those "Great effort!" stickers that littered their papers when they were younger. Think about the commendations these kids have received for doing nothing, or nothing but trying. Actual achievement, for years, was downplayed in favor of protecting delicate self-esteem.

The scariest result of all of this is that eventually the truth will out. Someone will be blatantly honest, and when it happens, it will be as if everyone else up to that point has lied. Because they have. We have raised a generation of teenagers who have been lied to their entire lives about their true abilities. We've told kids who couldn't carry a tune that they should sing in the upcoming talent show. We've made up stories about coaches and their favoritism to keep our kids from knowing they didn't make the team because they weren't good enough. We've justified our kids' job losses as poor placement or, worse, their being "better than that." And when our children did poorly in a class? The teacher was not a good fit for these children's learning styles.

It is difficult to reverse the damage done by false praise and protective justifications. If you had been raised to believe that all good things stem from your effort and all bad things stem from others' actions, you would have a pretty high opinion of yourself, too. But the damage can be abated during these years, and if you don't do damage control now, trust me, it will be ugly when your kids reach college or the workplace. During their high school years, they are still at home with you. They love you and appreciate your opinion, even if they act like they don't. If they are going to get bad news, better it should come from you than anyone else. So now is the time to start being honest. With real life looming just a few years away, you have a great excuse for your new approach to constructive criticism.

Nobody Is Perfect

It is important to make your kids comfortable with the fact that they are not perfect and you don't expect them to be. This should be a tremendous relief for all concerned, so there is nothing to fear here. What is more difficult is saying the words that let your children know they are not especially good at something, especially when they think they are.

When I was in high school, I was invited to participate in a competition that rewarded well-rounded young women. We competed in categories such as service, academics, talent, and communication skills. As I prepared my talent, I decided to sing and play the guitar. My mom, not wanting to hurt me by telling me that I really couldn't sing, instead suggested an instrumental piece. Her argument: I might get nervous up there on stage and it might cause my voice to quiver, so playing the guitar was a safer bet. I agreed and did just that. She had solved the problem temporarily and spared me embarrassment in that moment, but looking back, I really wish she had been honest with me. Yes, it probably would have hurt my feelings temporarily, but it would have saved me from years of putting myself in singing situations where I had no business being. I was never as bad as the *American Idol* rejects, but for a long time I deluded myself into thinking I had the voice of a canary when really it was more of a dying raccoon.

When I asked my mom, years later, why she never told me that I couldn't sing, her response was that she didn't want to hurt my feelings. But then I wondered, what else did she keep from me? That's what happens. When you lie to kids to protect them, and they finally realize it, they wonder what else you have lied about. They begin to question if you are honest with them when they ask you if they are smart, attractive, or easy to get along with. What begins as a gentle protection of your children's feelings can turn into a source of distrust in your relationship with your kids. They should always know that when they ask you something, you will be honest with them. There is no doubt in my mind that my mother's beliefs in me fueled my beliefs in my own abilities. I am sure that as parents, you have the same motive—to encourage and show faith in your kids' abilities, so that they, in turn, will believe in themselves. The intentions are wonderful, but be aware that they can backfire.

Times have changed since we were children. Back then, we knew our strengths and weaknesses because the other adults in our lives weren't afraid to be honest with us about them. Our teachers didn't coddle us, and our coaches didn't feed our egos. They never worried about mincing words and saw their jobs as telling us exactly where we stood in society. Our mothers could afford to be nice because everyone else in the world was fairly blunt. We got the grades we deserved, we got trophies only when we won big, and no one worried, particularly, about our self-esteem.

Nowadays you can safely assume you are the only one in your children's lives who will be completely honest with them. That makes this responsibility doubly important. While everyone else is protecting your children's self-esteem, you have to be the one to remind them that they are far from perfect. There are a few things you can do at this point, regardless of how you have handled things up until now, to help your children develop a true sense of worth based on real achievements. The flip side of that is that you must also help your children accept the fact that they have weaknesses, that their effort isn't always enough to achieve all they had hoped for, and that everyone is not a winner.

Imagine that Vince is applying to the National Honor Society. The lengthy application process requires a GPA of 3.8 or higher, demonstrated community service that amounts to no less than twenty hours, and three examples of leadership roles held during the high school years. Vince meets most of the requirements but not all of them. If Vince were your son, what would you tell him about applying?

- He should be perfectly honest on the application and submit it with hopes that his strengths might outweigh his weaknesses.
- He should not submit an application. He doesn't meet the minimum requirements, so doing so would be a waste of time.
- He should "fudge" his qualifications a little in order to meet the requirements.
- He should give you time to talk to the sponsor and see if consideration can be extended to admit him.

- He should talk to the sponsor and tell her all the reasons why he would be an asset to the organization.

The problem with the above options is that all of them can be justified in one way or another. That's what makes your job as parents so difficult. You could find a way to explain or excuse all of these choices, but it really comes down to the fact that Vince doesn't meet the minimum requirements. As parents who want to be honest with their kids while still encouraging them, your best choice would be the first one. In this scenario, you don't make Vince feel as if he is more qualified than he is, but you encourage him to try anyway. If he is rejected, he (a) understands why and accepts it, (b) learns what he has to do if he wants to make the club next year, and (c) still tries, because sometimes we get lucky.

Now, when Vince doesn't make the National Honor Society and is upset about it anyway, what do you do? Do you march to the school and demand a meeting with the sponsor? Do you go to the principal and complain about the unfairness of it all? Do you tell Vince that the teacher must not like him or is playing favorites? I've seen every one of these scenarios unfold, time and again. It happens every year, as a matter of fact. Rather than letting their children face the fact that they just were not qualified for an organization, parents will storm the front office (or the coach's office, or the teacher's classroom), demanding that the policies be changed to protect their children's egos. This is dangerous and does children no favors whatsoever.

Kids can have wonderful attributes and much to offer and still not be right for a class, a club, or a job. As adults, it happens to us all the time, and if we are emotionally healthy we accept it. As good as we may be, there is always—let's be honest—someone better. As hard as we try, sometimes we still cannot achieve what we wanted. As much as we want something, we don't always get it. Children need to learn this. And you are the only one who is going to teach it to them.

Building Realistic Self-Esteem

If you are looking for ways to build your children's self-esteem without feeding into overinflated egos, here are some steps you can take:

1. Always encourage your kids to move outside of their comfort zones. I said this in chapter 7 when I encouraged you to get your kids into at least one AP course. The same applies to other areas of their lives. Don't let them rest on their laurels. Instead, push them to try new hobbies, explore a variety of clubs, try out for different teams. If they are afraid to try something new, encourage them to at least dabble in it. Every time they overcome a fear or a discomfort, they prove to themselves that they can continue to overcome fears and discomforts. That is a priceless realization for everyone.

2. Try to get your kids interested in sports and hobbies that do not overinflate egos but provide internal motivation to improve. For instance, football players are constantly told that they are Big Men on Campus, to the point that just being on the team guarantees recognition. The swimmers, cross-country runners, and golfers? Not so much. These sports provide an opportunity for kids to consistently strive to top themselves, to better their time and improve their personal score. And when the athletes are recognized, it's because they won, because they achieved something great, not just because they showed up.

The same goes for hobbies and interests that bring tremendous personal satisfaction without a lot of hoopla, such as scouts, creative endeavors and contests, and chess and other games of skill.

3. Insist that your children participate in community service. The rewards are manifold. First, they will stop thinking about themselves for a few hours and begin to think of others. They will learn they are not the center of the universe. Second, they will realize how blessed they are in their own lives, not necessarily from anything they did but from what they have been given. Charity sparks gratitude. Third, it is unlikely they will get external rewards for their service. Instead, charity is something they do because it is the right thing to do. They will discover how much better that feels than any trophy they've been given.

4. Make your kids stick it out, no matter how difficult it may be. Don't let them quit jobs that are hard or that require them to do some tasks they find distasteful. Imagine if we adults did that! Since we know that life provides only so many options, and many options have negative aspects, we need to teach our children to be prepared for that reality.

5. Seek out coaches, teachers, and other youth leaders who hold kids accountable It is important that other adults in your children's lives reinforce the concept of taking responsibility for one's actions. Thank the leaders who don't go easy on your kids, and help them as much as you can to push kids to achieve. And if you can't find those kinds of leaders, become one. Offer to coach your kids' club teams or sponsor a group.

6. Tell your kids when they don't do something well at home. If they ask you, be honest with them. You can be as gentle or as blunt as you like, but tell them the truth. Chances are you have plenty of praise to heap on them and plenty of love in your heart for them. A few criticisms and suggestions will round out that love and make your compliments all the more precious.

7. Be honest with your kids, but do it from a place of love. Constructive criticism got its name from its inherent helpfulness. When criticism is given, it should be with the express purpose of helping children improve or become aware of areas where improvement should take place. It should not be to demean or put children in their place. Every child should be able to hear constructive criticism, use it to self-assess, and seek ways to improve. This is a sign of maturity, and you should see more of this as your teenagers grow and accept the fact that they are not always right and they are not perfect.

You may be wondering why all of this is so important. Well, aside from helping kids to know their value and worth, you are helping your children grow into contributing, self-aware members of society. The world does not need more people who have great self-esteem and no real talent—we have an overabundance of them already. What the world needs is people who know who they are and how they can contribute without expecting anything but personal satisfaction in return.

CHAPTER 10

Making Sure Teens Know That the Way They Look and Sound Matters

T WOULD BE NEARLY IMPOSSIBLE TO OVEREMPHASIZE THE impact of the media on teens' behavior and perceptions of reality. That reality includes dress, language, and the way kids choose to present themselves to others. For years now, we have watched boys' pants dip lower and grow baggier and girls' skirts and shorts rise higher and become tighter because that's how young men and women dress on TV and in movies. Children take their cues from what they are most surrounded by, and unfortunately, that's TV, movies, and music. Consider the slew of studies that have focused on teen body image and the overwhelming evidence that suggests unobtainable ideals stem from celebrities. Adolescents form many of their ideas about what their bodies should look like, how they should dress, what accessories they should wear, and so on, from the faces and bodies that relentlessly flash across their screens.

While actors, singers, and famous-just-for-being-famous icons set the fashion standard, kids are even more heavily influenced by their peers. Most kids want to look like their friends, period.

And don't fall under the misconception that boys are different from girls in this regard. Boys are equally concerned about their looks. While they strive for the "I just threw something on" look, in actuality their appearance is practiced and calculated. They actually care very much about their hair, their clothes, and their shoes and notice these things on one another. In the same way, girls judge girls. Hair, makeup, clothing, shoes, accessories—all play a part in determining personalities and choosing friends. To be honest, most kids do not dress for the opposite sex, they dress for their own sex. It's all about fitting in with peers and presenting a certain image.

Much like adults, kids choose social groups and friends based, at least initially, on looks. We all make judgments about people immediately upon meeting them, most of the time without even realizing it. Researchers from New York University found that we so subconsciously react to meeting someone for the first time that we make seven judgments about that person within the first eleven seconds of the meeting.[1] First impressions matter, and we need to teach this to our kids.

I do an entire unit on this concept with my students, in which we discuss the media's and society's influence on body image and judgments. I begin by describing three women with nothing but their physical characteristics, such as dress, hair, makeup, and accessories. I then ask my students to draw conclusions about the women based solely on these descriptions. Without hesitating, and without arguing, all of them, boys and girls alike, immediately categorize the women: The one with the long hair, long fingernails, and high heels is a girly-girl who likes to attract men. The one with the coiffed hair, simple makeup, dressed in the navy skirt and jacket is a professional. The one with no makeup, simply combed hair, and Birkenstocks is "one of those earthy women." Year after year, regardless of the composition of the students in class, the same conclusions are drawn. Readily, it is apparent to everyone that they have all judged these women within a minute of having them described. And the thing is, I could provide ten more descriptions of ten different men or women and we would all categorize them with little to no dissent in our judgments. It's eerily foolproof.

For a different unit about stereotypes, I flash photos of the famous and infamous on a screen. These celebrities, criminals, and other notable people enjoyed their renown well before my students were old enough to know who they are. I ask my kids to silently jot down notes about each person pictured and then share their thoughts. Immediately, stereotypes surface, as students associate dreadlocks with drugs, prim and proper clothing with religion, smart suits with wealth, and extremely casual dress with poverty. Sometimes they are dead on; other times they couldn't be more wrong.

Projecting an Image Through Personal Appearance

So what does this tell us? It tells us that clothes do project an image, good or bad. There is no denying that the way we dress, style our hair, and carry ourselves speaks, rightly or wrongly, of our persona. It means that if we wish to convey a certain image, or avoid conveying another image, the best way to do this, at least initially, is through our appearance and demeanor.

This is one of the reasons private schools often opt for uniforms over choice of dress. They know that judgments are made based on personal style and that dress reveals a great deal about people. In order to level the playing field, they attempt to erase indicators of socioeconomic backgrounds, as well as eliminate problems with dress-code violations and distractions due to clothing. That's how much personal appearance matters. It's a distraction, it's a basis for judgment, and it's a revealer of personality.

Kids know this, and at a very young age. It is why they hit you up to take them to expensive stores that sell cool, hip, or sexy images. I'm thinking of one retail clothing chain in particular whose chief executive officer infamously admitted that it markets exclusively to good-looking people. This comment shouldn't have shocked anyone, given the fact that the company makes no pretense about featuring impossibly gorgeous models, including live ones who stand outside store entrances to pull impressionable young customers in. After purchases are made, merchandise is placed in bags featuring sexy men and women much older than the target audience to show them what they can be if they continue to shop at that store. Those bags announce to the world that the merchandise inside will turn good-looking teens into even more desirable, sexy adults. Keep in mind that not only teens but prepubescent children are drawn to this type of marketing. The earlier you can teach your kids to avoid these image-endorsing labels, the easier it will be to help them dress appropriately as they get older.

Your kids are fully aware of fashion. They value it and will spend huge sums of money (yours) to acquire it. They notice what their peers are wearing, and they judge them accordingly. So if they try to tell you otherwise, don't believe them. I see them every day, and I watch them interact. They know the popular fashions and they care about them. It's interesting, then, that teens will argue with you interminably that their appearance doesn't matter. It's an incredible paradox that they hope you won't notice. On the one hand, their image means more to them than almost anything else. On the other hand, they will claim that it shouldn't make a difference how they dress, Grandma shouldn't care if they pierce their lip, and a tattoo sleeve will not in any way impede their future careers.

How they present themselves to the world may be one of the most crucial decisions they make in their lifetimes, and they will make this decision over and over again. Please, don't allow them to get a pass just because they are teenagers.

If there is one thing that drives me absolutely nuts, it is when parents permit their children to wear anything they want, regardless of the inappropriateness, and then shake their heads in defeat and claim they have no control over it. Um, yes you do. Even if your children buy all their own clothes (which I doubt), you still have the power to refuse certain outfits, to have them returned to the store, until your children realize you will not allow them to dress inappropriately. This includes scanty, barely-there outfits, clothing with gang affiliations or "thug" connotations, and clothing with references to alcohol, drugs, and sex. There is a wide variation of choices out there to allow kids to express themselves as individuals, but these inappropriate choices need to be taken off the table while you still have some control over their dress.

Your hope, in doing this, is that you will teach your kids a valuable lesson about dressing appropriately for a venue, presenting themselves the way they need to for the opportunity, and being aware of and respecting social mores. Children need to know that there are certain ways to dress for school, church, sporting events, fine restaurants, and job interviews. Shorts, a T-shirt, and a baseball cap cut it in only one of those venues.

Your kids will—if they haven't done so already—tell you they have to dress a certain way to fit in at school. This will be based on how their friends or potential friends dress, and their acceptance is crucial to them. So it is okay to indulge them, to a certain extent, in this area, as long as their clothing is age and venue appropriate. When it begins to cross the line, however, you should take the opportunity to teach them about what is absolutely not acceptable. I have met with parents who have explained they hate the way their kids dress, but their kids insist all their friends dress that way. This conversation takes place at school, where parents have walked down the hallway to get to my room and passed fifty teenagers along the way. They can see for themselves that everyone most certainly does not dress like their children. It's no different from the "But everyone does this, Mom!" argument you hear time and time again. It's just not true, and you know that. I primarily hear this argument regarding boys in low-slung, baggy pants and boxer shorts. I've taught in all types of schools with kids from every culture and socioeconomic background, and I'm here to tell you that most boys do not dress like gangsters. There is a select group that does, just like there is a select group of jocks, preps, nerds, and theater kids. All of these groups exist, just as they did when you were children. Your children are going to naturally gravitate to one of these groups, and there is not a whole lot you can do about it. But if you don't approve of the "dress code" that group has adopted, you certainly have some say about that. Even boys who want to wear their pants hanging off their butts (which, by the way, violates most schools' dress codes) can compromise by wearing loose jeans that still fit and sit at the waist.

In the same way, if your daughter expects to wear tight, short skirts, you can allow her to wear skirts to satisfy the girly-girl in her but insist they be no more than a couple of inches above the knee. You can permit a snug top but forbid a see-through one. There are many ways to compromise and allow choice but still set parameters for acceptable dress. Allow your children to choose and dress according to their own personal style but insist they retain tasteful boundaries.

The major lesson to be learned is that personal style is personal because it reflects who your children are, so they need to think long and hard about what they want to project to others. They will fight you relentlessly, and you will need to work hard to remain consistent, but it will be worth it in the long run.

You might be wondering if teachers judge students by their

appearance, and the simple answer is that we are human and do exactly what you do. The good news is that those of us who have been in this business a long time realize that appearances can be deceiving. I had a male student who wore all black, heavy chains, black lipstick, and multiple piercings that always landed him in the principal's office. He remains one of my favorite students of all time because he had a heart of gold and was a big ol' softy. Unfortunately, there was only one store in the mall that would hire him for a summer job, and most people disliked him on sight. He turned people off. He scared people. As unfair as that was, it didn't matter, because that was the reality he had created for himself.

Likewise, I have taught girls who obsessed over their looks and primped in class, applying lipstick and spritzing themselves with perfume. I had one female student who actually attempted to paint her nails in my class. Girls who do this go out of their way to up their attractiveness quotient, but the message they send is, "I don't care about intellectual pursuits or internal beauty. All that matters is how I appear to others." The reality is that for many of them, that just isn't true. They are smart and they have great substance, but it is masked by an overemphasis on looking beautiful and conveying a superficial image.

Let me pause here to focus on girls for a minute. Over recent years—again, I blame this on reality TV and movie characters— girls have gotten the idea that looks are everything and being ditzy is somehow cute or sexy. They have dumbed down. They will give the most ridiculous answers and ask silly questions that suggest they are dumber than a box of rocks. One on one, however, they are bright and inquisitive and way smarter than they let on in front of their peers. This has to stop. If I recognize it, I call them on it immediately via a private conversation after class. But this conversation really needs to take place at home, and the earlier the better.

As parents, you need to send the message, regularly, that your girls are valued not for their looks but for their inner beauty and personal accomplishments. Value their intelligence by praising them for intellectual pursuits and placing emphasis on areas other than looks, and do this often. Keep in mind that you have a true war to fight to overcome the images that bombard them in the media. Every single day, in countless ways, girls are told that looks and sexuality determine their worth. So you need to combat that directly, both in the way you talk to your daughters and the way you talk about them to others. When you talk to grandparents and friends, especially in front of your daughters, talk about their accomplishments and achievements, not about how cute they looked in the dress they wore to school. Concentrate on strengths and character and the aspects of life your daughters can actually control. When you do this, girls actually do take control of their lives, a pivotal change that marks the beginning of adulthood.

Before we move on to areas of demeanor and etiquette, let's pause to summarize areas of focus regarding appearance:

- Teach your kids that there is a difference between obsessing about looks and understanding the role appearance plays in others' judgment of them. Yes, they should dress to reflect their personal style. But yes, they also have a responsibility to dress appropriately for various occasions.

- Kids love being independent and having choices. Establish parameters and then give them freedom to experiment within those boundaries. They may not dress to your taste, and that's okay. Allow them to be their own people with their own sense of fashion. This is an important step in establishing their own identities.

- Teach them that dressing appropriately is a sign of respect to others. Everything is not about them, as I've said many times, and this is yet another example. Out of respect for their grandmother, they should remove the piercings. Out of respect for the church environment, they should dress with some sense of reverence. Out of respect for interviewers, they should dress professionally. And so on, and so on. The ability to recognize expectations and to adapt accordingly is one of the most important teachable skills for future success.

- Always emphasize internal worth, including intellect, kindness, sensitivity, and personal strengths, over external appearance. This should make your fight a little less tiresome as kids place less emphasis on their clothing and more on their individual pursuits.

- Shop according to your budget, not according to kids' demands for labels and designer clothing and accessories. Do not fall prey to their arguments that everyone dresses a certain way. They don't, and I can guarantee you that your kids can dress similarly and fit in with their peers just fine without bankrupting you.

Demeanor and Etiquette

Beyond clothing, how young adults carry themselves and conduct themselves around others is paramount to making good impressions and achieving desired results. When kids apply for their first jobs, they must demonstrate maturity and a willingness to work. When they go to dinner at a nice restaurant, they must present themselves as people relatively accustomed to fine dining. When they talk to the principal, they must make eye contact and show some deference to an authority figure. When they get pulled over for a traffic violation, they must know how to speak respectfully to the police officer. Every single day, how they have been taught to act matters.

All kids should be instructed from their earliest years that when introduced to an adult, they must make eye contact, shake hands firmly, smile, and say, "It's nice to meet you." When they go to a friend's home, they should say hello to parents before disappearing to hang out. Likewise, before leaving their friend's home, they should thank parents for having them over and wish them a good day. They should not ask for food or help themselves to another's fridge or pantry. They should understand boundaries and personal space, and respect them.

The way that kids address adults is also important. Kids should call adults what they wish to be called, always starting with titles, such as Ms. or Mr., unless they are told otherwise. Even if an adult says your children can call her by her first name, you might want to teach your children to make it slightly more respectful by calling her Ms. Susan, for example. Most kids are uncomfortable calling adults by their first names, and believe it or not, the simple addition of a title can alter the dynamic enough that respect becomes the expectation. It also teaches children to avoid becoming too casual with those in higher positions. It's never a good idea to address the new boss as Bob when he fully expects to be called Mr. Smith. Children should be taught to play it safe by always defaulting to respectful exchanges, unless and until they are told otherwise.

When you are out with your kids, treat every experience as a teachable moment. If you haven't worked with your kids in these areas, you have only a couple of years left before you set them loose into the adult world. They will be expected to know how to conduct themselves. They will attend functions with professors or employers where they will be expected to dress nicely, have basic table manners, speak articulately, and follow the proper social mores for such situations. How they handle themselves in these situations can affect not only others' immediate perceptions of them but also their future opportunities.

A PERSONAL CASE IN POINT

As a college student, my son, Jonathan, wanted to land a summer internship that would make him more marketable upon graduation. After putting together a resume and drafting an email, he reached out to local companies of interest. Their process of narrowing down potential hires from a large pool of applicants began with an exchange that tested applicants' abilities to communicate effectively via email. If Jonathan had used the lowercase *i* to refer to himself, or his email had been riddled with texting language or grammatical errors, the exchange would have stopped there. I can guarantee you that most applicants moved no further because their initial communication showed a lack of maturity and effort. Teach your kids to write with strong consideration of their audience and to speak properly and correctly in any and all communication.

Next, an interview was scheduled. Jonathan wore a freshly pressed suit, dress shoes, and a tie, which was appropriate for an economics internship. Had he applied for a job as a truck driver, I still would have encouraged him to wear khaki pants and a polo shirt, simply because that is what is appropriate for an interview. As a high school student, he dressed this way for an interview for a job at a burger joint; not only did he get the job but they put him on the catering schedule because his dress suggested he could do more. The mantra in our house has always been, "Dress for what you want to be." Jeans or shorts are not appropriate for interviews, no matter what the position may be. Teach your kids to dress more nicely than the job requires, especially during the interview, and then adjust accordingly once the job is secure.

We all know the rules of interviewing, but you would be shocked at the number of kids who do not know how to handle themselves when they are face to face with adults. If you have taught your kids the importance of eye contact and a handshake, this will be second nature to them, and that's exactly what you want. As nervous as Jonathan was to interview for that important position, he walked into the interview with the confidence of someone who had known how to conduct himself in front of adults for years. His clothes, neat haircut, and overall demeanor suggested a young man who would be an asset to the company, someone they could introduce to others with pride. Make no bones about it, that is important to companies.

And then there was the most important part of the interview, the actual conversation. You probably are well aware of the horrible speech patterns teenagers have adopted over the last ten years. In any given conversation, how many times do your children use the word *like*, as in, "I, like, couldn't believe that he, like, kept talking, after the teacher, like, told him, like, a hundred times to, like, stop!" Whenever I have my students talk in front of the class, I make them aware of the extent to which this has become a problem. They listen for it and are stunned at the number of times their peers use the word *like*. Sometimes, just to make a point, they will record the number for a friend. Forty-some "likes" in a five-minute speech or presentation is not entirely uncommon. Now take those same kids and put them in an unrehearsed situation, such as an interview, in which they are nervous and unsure of themselves. Imagine how many "likes," "you knows," and "I means" will pepper their conversation, and imagine how that will sound to an adult. I realize you cannot interrupt every conversation they have with you, but make it your mission to point this out to them and work with them on eliminating these filler words from their speech. I'm sure part of Jonathan's ability to land the internship had to do with his speech and the way he articulated his thoughts. It is crucial that you work with your kids on their vocabulary and oral expression.

A brief aside about something that often applies to girls and their speech habits: In recent years, girls have started turning every declarative sentence into a question. They raise the intonation of their voices toward the end of the sentence, thereby making every statement sound like a question. The effect is that the speaker appears unsure of herself, like she is afraid that what she is saying is wrong and she is doubting its validity. Listen to your kids, particularly your daughters, to see if they have fallen into that habit, and point it out to them. It's important that young adults' speech convey confidence and assuredness.

Presenting Themselves Well in Every Way, Every Day

Once Jonathan landed the internship, the real test came in his day-to-day behavior and the way he conducted himself on a regular basis. But he would never have gotten the chance to prove himself if he had not presented himself well at the outset. He beat out a number of applicants for the position based on first impressions and a one-hour conversation. Your kids will find themselves in that exact same position many, many times in their lives. They need to be prepared in every possible way, including their outward appearance, mannerisms, and ability to conduct thoughtful conversations.

They will also need to tweak or completely overhaul their online presence to present themselves as trustworthy, hard-working individuals whom companies and universities should trust. As I discussed earlier, Facebook and other forms of social media have become just as important in admissions and hiring decisions as a candidate's background. The Equal Employment Opportunity Commission (EEOC) reports that in 2011, 75 percent of recruiters were instructed to do online research of candidates, so as I said in chapter 7, there is nothing private about social media.[2] But brace yourself for this next fact from the EEOC: Seventy percent of recruiters *reject* candidates based on what they discover online. In this competitive market, no one can afford to lose a job or college admission over a hastily posted tweet or Instagram status or photo. Caution your kids, from as young an age as possible, that everything they post online is visible to everyone. Ask them how they would feel if their religious leaders, grandparents, and future bosses could access everything they have shared through social media. Then assure them that all these people can.

Jonathan's job ended with an invitation to a fancy restaurant with the boss. Again, he had to know how to conduct himself in this situation, and it had to be taught to him ahead of time. Everything from the etiquette of ordering to placing a napkin on his lap to taking smaller bites and not talking with food in his mouth had been taught to him over the many years preceding this important night. Don't neglect these duties as unimportant. They are actually exceedingly important because they all play a part in painting a picture of your children. If you think about the endless opportunities your children have to either impress or disgust other people, the numbers are staggering. Manners matter. And they will continue to matter for the rest of your children's lives.

Now that your children have entered their teen years, you can take them virtually anywhere and teach them about proper dress and behavior at any number of varying establishments. If your children are doing things you have never done—attending college, planning white-collar careers, or interviewing for certain types of jobs with which you have no experience—reach out to friends, family members, and even the Internet for guidelines for these situations. You can find YouTube videos that teach virtually anything, and kids are happy to use them as nonthreatening tutorials on life skills.

Most important, make your kids observers of the world around them. Teach them to take in their surroundings and to pick up social cues from people in the know. What an incredible skill for them to learn, and how helpful it will be as they move through life's unfamiliar situations. You have the power to effect these changes, and believe me, your children will thank you later.

CHAPTER 11

Getting Kids Organized: A Strong Foundation for a Lifetime of Success

IMAGINE THAT YOU HAVE BEEN PARTNERED WITH A COL-league at work to complete an important project for your company. Your bonus, your standing in the company, and your reputation all ride on your ability to work together to optimize your business. Your partner, Mark, is known for flying by the seat of his pants. He rarely writes anything down, he procrastinates, and sometimes he misses deadlines entirely. Determined to make the partnership successful, you develop a schedule for completing tasks and set a meeting with Mark to discuss the plan. He shows up fifteen minutes late and takes no notes, swearing he will remember everything you discuss. You delegate responsibilities but know he will forget half of them by the time he walks out the door. He misses checkpoints along the way and waits until the night before the project is due to begin putting it together. At that point, he frantically calls you to cover for him, throws together a haphazard presentation, and the next morning arrives late, disheveled and groggy from a late night of scrambling.

How do you feel about the fact that you had to rely on someone like Mark to get the job done? Are you bitter about his selfishness and inability to think about how his actions affect others? Are you frustrated that a grown man could be so disorganized? Are you wondering how long he will keep his job before everyone tires of his irresponsibility?

Disorganization is prevalent in large part because many people are not taught organizational skills at a young age. You may expect your teenagers to naturally pick up on these skills as they progress through school, but to be honest, most schools do not teach organization. At the high school level, teachers are consumed with imparting lengthy subject matter and rarely have time to instruct on good study habits. If your children don't know how to plan ahead, keep track of responsibilities, and prioritize, they will feel the pain from these deficiencies in every area of their lives. And don't think they will hurt only themselves. Throughout high school they will be expected to work with partners or in groups where their participation is crucial not only to their own learning but to others'. Disorganization affects every area of life, consistently hurts children, and greatly impacts future success.

With high schoolers, disorganization can be especially harmful. When kids don't stay on top of their assignments, they resort to shortcuts, and those shortcuts generally involve, at the least, irresponsible use of the Internet, and at the worst, cheating. When kids don't keep track of their meetings and practices, they arrive late and unprepared, if they arrive at all. As a result, disorganization can lead to zeroes on assignments, restrictions from playing in the next game, or expulsion from clubs or activities.

Let's look at some specific ways disorganization can lead to unwanted behaviors and dire consequences.

CASE IN POINT

Patti has a project due one week from today. *That project isn't due for another week,* she thinks to herself. *I have other things to do in the meantime, and I'll get to that sometime next week.* Days pass and it is now two days before the due date. Patti has barely given the project a thought, and when the teacher mentions it in class, she is struck with her first twinge of worry. *Better get on that tonight,* she thinks. *Gotta get that done and not wait until the last minute.*

That night, she reviews the requirements with a new sense of dread. There is more involved than she originally thought, including research into three sources. But the Internet makes everything easier, in her mind, so she hits the web, quickly choosing the first three sources she encounters. She copies and pastes the source information into a new document, adds a few words of her own to round them out, and calls it a night.

The next day, she overhears her friends talking about the project. Amanda, who has straight As in all her classes and has been dubbed the group's genius, complains about the three hours she spent analyzing data and the conclusions she drew. Patti asks Amanda to email her the paper so she can get some ideas for her own analysis, and Amanda acquiesces. That night, Patti copies and pastes Amanda's work, changes a few words and sentences around, and considers her project complete.

Just before she is set to go to bed, she gets a frantic call from her friend Elyse. "Patti! Oh my God, this project is ridiculous! Can you help me?"

"Sure," Patti replies, "what do you need?"

"Can you take a picture of your paper and send it to me? I need to see what someone else has done so I know if I'm doing this right."

Patti agrees, snaps some photos of her paper, and texts them to Elyse. She feels that doing so means she is a good friend, and she knows Elyse will help her out on future assignments. She rests easily and is happy to turn in the project the next day.

A week later, projects are returned, and Patti stares in disbelief at an F, boldly scrawled at the top of her project. As she leafs through the paper, first resentfully, then with increasing nervousness, she digests the following comments from her teacher:

"These sources are not valid or reliable. One is a blog by a teenager. One is Wiki Answers, and the third is an online magazine geared toward children. The third source is not nearly sophisticated enough for a high school research project. How much time did you spend finding sources?"

"This analysis looks familiar. I doubt that two students using entirely different sources could come up with the same analysis."

"These sentences don't sound like you. They are written in a completely different style from the rest of your paper."

"I saw these exact sentences in another student's paper. How did that happen?"

In addition to these pointed questions, her teacher has circled typos and grammatical mistakes on every page of the paper. In her haste, Patti had forgotten to edit or proofread, expecting spell check and grammar check to alert her to any mistakes. Her rush to complete a weeklong project in two nights led her to cut corners, make dangerous academic moves such as plagiarizing and copying a friend's work, and turn in sloppy work. Her grade has just taken a huge hit, and she will struggle to pull it up for the rest of the semester.

Problems Caused by Lack of Organization

The problem with disorganization is that it not only produces a messy desk and missed deadlines, but it also sets children up for desperate actions, such as cheating. Kids say they don't have time to study, so they resort to cheat sheets on tests. They say they don't have time to do all their math problems, so they split them with their friends and then copy each other's work. They say they don't have time to read through all those Google sources, so they accept the information they find immediately as true and accurate. Beyond the obvious and immediate repercussions of this rushed approach to learning is the long-term harm that results from an inability to discern fact from fiction.

First, kids are often highly misinformed about any number of subjects because they don't take the time to locate valid sources. In seeking answers to questions, not only do they not think but they accept the first answer—no matter how inaccurate—provided to them. They use unfounded information from the results they see in their web searches to help form their political alliances, their religious convictions, and various aspects of their worldview. Think about how frightening this is. We are raising an entire generation of people who get their answers and belief systems from ignorant, biased strangers who are uploading fallacies from the comfort of their Barcaloungers.

Second, children seem to have no compunctions about taking any shortcut to a solution, including cheating. They don't call it that, of course. They call it "sharing information," and they have convinced themselves that there is absolutely nothing wrong with it. To their way of thinking, if they can complete their work in half the time, why not? If they have an edge going into the test, why shouldn't they grab it? If they are able to complete a major project in a couple of hours by cutting corners, then doesn't that just make them more efficient? This is their thought process, and it is getting them into trouble and depriving them of true learning. They have convinced themselves that they can do it all, when in actuality they are doing nothing but stealing other people's ideas.

As an English teacher, I watch kids struggle with reading a book independently. Their first inclination is almost always to read the online summaries instead. These summaries are dry and sometimes completely erroneous. Since their sole function is to provide just the facts, Jack, they are not even enjoyable to read. But kids will choose them over beautifully written, entertaining books because the books are longer. They will then regurgitate the online summary information on essays and tests, completely depriving themselves of the joy and discovery of reading, of interpreting, and of drawing their own conclusions. Many don't believe in their ability to process difficult language or more challenging works because they have never taken the time to work through these texts. This belief feeds on itself over the years, so that juniors and seniors reveal to me that they have never actually read a required book. When I tell them my quizzes and tests are designed so that students must read the novels, not the summaries, they are terrified.

When those tests come, therefore, students have no qualms about revealing test questions to other students in an effort to help them. It should come as no surprise that if only one version of a test is given, the kids who take it at the end of the day will invariably do better than the kids who took it first. Teenagers will do anything to help their friends out, including sharing test questions and answers. Even if there is a curve and they will be negatively affected by students who score higher, they will continue to follow the teenage code of having each other's backs.

Some take this to the extreme. I once found a cheat sheet in the hood of a student's sweatshirt. It wasn't doing him any good at all, but the kid who sat behind him had found the perfect method—he thought—for cheating. When I caught him, the kid insisted that the holder of the cheat sheet knew nothing about it, again covering for his friend.

When cell phones became popular, cheating took on a life of its own. Now it is possible for students to snap shots of tests and instantly send them out en masse. Some particularly enterprising students complete tests, snap photos of the answers, and sell them to kids who "didn't have time to study." Other kids find ways to cheat on their own. Hiding answers on cell phones or writing them on desks or body parts is common practice for kids who are willing to cheat. One kid kept extra loose-leaf paper on his desk during a quiz. When I walked by, I noticed that the paper looked different in some way. Stopping to hold it up to the light, I discovered that the student had previously written the answers on another piece of paper, pressing heavily with his pencil so the supposedly blank page that had been under it now had an imprint of the answers. Nothing was actually written on the paper, but it contained all the answers in the imprint. Ingenious? Maybe, but it just goes to show how far kids will go to cover for their lack of organization and effort.

Children find themselves turning to these desperate measures because they wait until the last minute to do everything. They are unable to clarify assignments or ask for extra help from the teacher because they wait until the night before an assignment is due to begin work on it. Schools are providing more resources than ever, but students don't take advantage of them, because they don't plan ahead. For instance, I taught in a school that had a full-time writing center staffed by English teachers. Students could schedule conferences with these teachers to get help with essays and receive feedback on areas for improvement. They could walk in at any time, during study halls or lunch, for instance, without an appointment and without taking up any time outside of the regular school day. Yet most students never used this resource. Not only did they fail to plan this one step, but they failed to plan, period.

What is truly intriguing is that children have a tool at their disposal twenty-four hours a day that they could use to plan, schedule, and keep track of all of their appointments: their cell phones. That one device can serve them in many capacities, including calendar scheduling and personalized reminders. The problem is that of all the capabilities built into a smartphone, kids rarely use this feature. The reason is mostly psychological and quite astounding.

Kids think of their cell phones as serving two purposes: making their lives easier and entertaining them. If a phone feature doesn't appear to them to meet one of those needs, the feature simply goes unused. In a survey I conducted with my students, I found that the primary uses for a cell phone are, in descending order:

1. Texting
2. Communicating via social media
3. Making calls (infrequently, but still a necessity)
4. Playing games
5. Taking photos
6. Surfing the web
7. Navigating to unknown locations

Of all the kids I spoke with, only a handful used their phone calendar. When I questioned this, the response shocked me: "We love our phones and have fun with them. The last thing we want to do is make them into work tools." Kids don't want to ruin their images of their phones by associating them with school. To them, phones are social status indicators and high-end toys for enjoyment. Children have no desire to change that image to include work reminders and assignment due dates. So even though they are fully aware they have the capability to plug all their assignments, due dates, sports games, club meetings, and so on into the one possession they have with them at all times, they won't do it.

Helping Your Children Get Organized

Therefore, the old-school method of organizing one's life must prevail. Make sure your children have a journal, notebook, agenda, or planner that exists solely for the purpose of getting organized. Most public schools provide a student handbook that contains a calendar with plenty of room to write down everything going on in even the busiest children's lives. Usually, the calendar is broken down into class periods so students can record individual assignments and due dates by subject. Make your children use this tool! Do not let them convince you that "it's all up here" while they point to their heads. It's not. Not even remotely. Some kids are better than others at remembering what they have to do, but none of them are good enough to remember the details for multiple classes and activities. Teach them now to write everything down the minute they hear it. If kids adjusted their behavior in only this one small way, the number of missed assignments and meetings and the instances of misremembered instructions would drop exponentially.

Once they have this tool and begin using it, keep their calendar full. One would think that the busier children get, the less organized they would become, but it's just not true. Have you ever heard the expression, "If you want something done, give it to a busy person"? Great truth lies in that aphorism. Kids get more organized when they have multiple items on their plate, simply because they have to be organized to keep track of their various responsibilities. They don't have a choice—they either write things down, scratch things off lists, and prioritize, or they don't accomplish any of their goals. When they can't play in the important game because they were late to practice, they quickly learn to finish their homework earlier so they can hit the road. When they let down their fellow club members by not fulfilling their role, they are embarrassed and secretly chastise themselves. The next time, they are more inclined to plan in advance.

Busy kids find a way to balance their lives, and that way is through organization. Beware, though, of overburdening your children with too many activities. A sport, a couple of clubs that meet monthly, and a weekly responsibility are usually ample to keep kids active without exhausting them. If their class work is suffering because they are tired or don't have the time to complete their work, pull back and continue to monitor. At this age, teenagers are capable of letting you know what they can handle.

But they cannot do this if no one ever teaches them how to organize their time. If they are kept busy, they will see the need for organization and strive to master it. If they are left to their own devices, their only responsibility being school, they won't use their time to become better students. Instead, they will use it to play video games, watch silly cat tricks on YouTube, and post their latest selfies to SnapChat. So do them a favor by insisting they get involved in a balance of activities outside of school. The benefits have been discussed throughout this book, but an added benefit is that it will force your kids to get organized.

That's where you come in. Organization is not an organic response; it is a learned behavior that must be practiced repeatedly until it eventually becomes second nature. Your goal is to get your kids to the place in which they wake up thinking, *What can I do today that will make my life a little easier tomorrow?* You want them to look forward, to project to a week from now, a month from now, and even four years from now, when they will graduate from high school and begin to make some of the biggest decisions in their lifetime. A teenager's inclination is to live in the moment, to think only of the here and now. You must teach your children to think everything through and to consider that every choice they make today will have implications and consequences tomorrow.

Here are some organizational techniques you can use to teach your children to prepare not only for tomorrow but for well into the future:

- **Keep a family calendar where everyone can record events and activities.** This serves several purposes. First, you will model good organization for your children. Let them see you finish a phone call with the doctor's office and immediately record your upcoming appointment. Let them see you consulting the calendar with your spouse to arrange an upcoming social event. Let them observe as you check the calendar before leaving the house for the day, confirming where you need to be and when you need to be there. Second, you will remind children that they are part of a family unit in which all cylinders must be firing for the unit to function properly. Their activities are not the only activities; Mom and Dad are just as busy, with full schedules of their own. When they realize this, they will, hopefully, become more considerate of everyone's time and more conscious of the role they play in the family dynamic.
- **Insist that your children keep an individual calendar for school assignments and activities that are unique to them.** This calendar should be their responsibility entirely. If they claim not to know what is due when, direct them to their calendars. If they haven't written their agenda down, they should be held accountable for

whatever consequences ensue. As they progress through high school, they must learn to take ownership of their responsibilities without their parents reminding them.

- **Teach your kids how to break down large assignments into manageable parts that are then spread out and tackled each night.** Instead of hounding them or doing their work for them because they waited until the last minute, set up checkpoints along the way and monitor their progress. Teach and prod when it comes to good study habits, but never do the work for them. Make sure they know what tools and resources are available to them, such as writing centers, online tutorials, homework helplines, library resources, and peer tutors. Provide these tools and then fully expect them to use them to reach their goals.

- **Help them come up with a plan as soon as they are given assignments.** Most are due the next day, so you will not need to involve yourself, but some are long range and would benefit greatly from advanced planning. Help your children pace themselves and discover the joy of completing a task early enough to actually have time to improve it.

- **Allow them to have a space that they organize exactly as they wish.** When it comes to their bedrooms and their own personal spaces, remember that your idea of organization likely differs from theirs. There is often a method to their madness, and your attempts to put order to their clothes, toiletries, and work space will usually end in mass confusion and anger targeted directly at your good intentions. Their room should be the one space that is exactly the way they want it (minus inappropriate or offensive decorations or materials). Their system doesn't need to make sense to you; believe it or not, most know exactly where everything is in that mess they call their rooms. If it makes you crazy, keep the door closed so you don't have to look at it.

- **Make consideration of others an organizational priority.** Your children must always respond to your texts or pick up the phone when you call (in exchange, you promise to keep this to a minimum). They must thank their grandparents for gifts soon after receiving them, before they have a chance to forget to show their gratitude. They must notify you of events that require your participation or presence as soon as they find out about them, and if they don't, they have no right to be upset or angry if you are unable to attend. Teach them that consideration of others' time is another good reason to be organized.

- **Emphasize prioritizing.** What are the most important tasks that must be completed today? What can wait a while? Back off or step in as kids demonstrate their understanding, or lack thereof, of priorities. Give more freedom as kids become more responsible, until organization becomes the expectation.

- **Make kids be responsible for remembering what they need for school, sports, and activities.** Run home for forgotten cleats, musical instruments, or homework one or two times, but not a third or fourth. Let them know it is their job to be prepared. They want you to see them as mature, responsible, and trustworthy, and as you loosen the reins, most kids will run with the challenge.

- **Have them lay everything out for their school day the night before.** They should select outfits, pack lunches, organize backpacks, and double-check that they have all assignments before going to bed each night. Morning is for getting dressed and eating breakfast, not last-minute dashes for items that should have been secured the night before.

- **Don't let your kids leave late for school or any of their other activities for any reason.** If they will not get out of bed in the morning, take away a prized possession until they consistently wake up by their own alarms and get to school on time. If they are tardy to school because their friends are late picking them up, don't allow them to ride with their friends anymore. If they drive and are late to school simply because they didn't allot enough time, make them ride the bus. Make it clear that if they are disorganized to the point of not meeting their responsibilities, you will take measures to ensure that they find ways to become more responsible.

- **Stress the importance of turning in assignments on time.** Teachers everywhere agree that deadlines should be enforced, but their hands are tied when parents and administrators pressure them to take late work. A growing movement in American education, formulated and furthered by helicopter parents, is to adopt no-penalty policies for late work. Since administrators and school boards don't want to deal with this increasing pressure from parents, they have given in to the point that deadlines and due dates carry no weight whatsoever. Don't be a demanding helicopter parent. Back teachers up when they insist kids meet deadlines. Reinforce this at home by giving your kids deadlines to complete chores. Consider all the times you must meet one deadline or another on any given day, and teach your children that this is a vital life skill.

- **Help your children plan for their futures by supporting them as they research and visit colleges, build high school resumes, work during summers, and participate in community service.** Set the tone and expectation that every year of high school should be about planning for the future, whether that future is college, trade school, the military, or the workforce. You can do this by helping your children find mentors, explore careers, pursue interests, and even job shadow.

If you are unorganized yourself, you know how much this weakness can affect every area of your life. If you've ever had to work with someone like Mark, who was never taught to organize and whose story opened our chapter, you know how much you can be affected by someone else's lack of organization. If your children have adopted Patti's tendencies to procrastinate and cut corners, it is possible they have also engaged in unethical behaviors such as cheating or plagiarizing. You can turn this around and teach your children to become organized and productive while you still have some control over the matter. Take the opportunity now to make their lives—and everyone's around them—better organized and more productive.

CHAPTER 12

How to Prepare Your Teens for Adulthood

ACCORDING TO A NEW PEW RESEARCH CENTER ANALY-sis, over one-third of adults ages eighteen to thirty-one still live at home with their parents.[1] Kids are delaying growing up and becoming independent, so that twenty-five is the new twenty, thirty is the new twenty-five, and so on. We've seen this happening for some time. Your parents may have married at eighteen years of age and begun having children shortly thereaf-ter. You probably married in your early twenties and were having babies in your late twenties. Looking at your teens right now, can you imagine them marrying in a couple of years? Chances are you can't.

What happened during this time span such that children seem to be maturing more slowly, are less capable of making major decisions, and are living at home much longer than they had in the past? And is this good or bad?

Let's discuss the good first. I think we are all grateful that kids are waiting until they have grown up a bit before choos-ing a life partner and having children. Even if we are still hap-pily married today, we can appreciate that we have changed tremendously since we were eighteen. We were kids, in a lot of ways, and underprepared for what life was about to throw at us. Somehow—really, quite inexplicably—some of us have remained married despite our having chosen spouses at a young age. It can be done, but we probably prefer that our kids wait a little longer before entering into that lifetime commitment.

Most parents today are vocal about their plans for their kids, and none of their plans includes a spouse or child anytime soon. The vast majority of parents expect their kids to go to college, and the rest are sending their kids off to the military or work. That is their hope, anyway, and I'm sure it is your hope as well. But when you look at your teens, do you see burgeoning young adults ready to become fully independent? Do you see men and women willing to take on any job necessary to provide for themselves?

Those in this generation are rarely ready for the real world by the time they become legal adults, so it is a good thing they are postponing marriage and children. But do you want them to also postpone the responsibility they need to gain their independence? I can't imagine that doing so is good for anyone involved, including society as a whole. If your job as parents is to raise self-sufficient individuals who will contribute positively to society, you're not doing a very good job if those individuals won't leave their childhood bedrooms.

In the seventeen years I have been a teacher, I have seen children become less and less responsible with each passing year. The helicopter and lawnmower parents I mentioned in chapter 3 have played a critical role in creating a generation of kids who let their parents handle everything. Cell phones have tied kids to their parents and provided easy access to answers and solutions that have nothing to do with children's independent thoughts or problem-solving skills. Schools have become havens of hand holding, repositories of retakes, and savers of self-esteem. Outside group play and ingenuity have been replaced with solitary activities and video games. The world is a very different place from the one we knew as children, and all of these factors have contributed to a generation of dependency.

Indulge me for a moment as I mention two other huge contributors to the problem: the movie and television industries and what they have passed off as teenage entertainment in recent years. Here's a challenge for you: Try to think of one popular "clean" comedy geared to teenagers in the last ten years. Having trouble thinking of even one? Now look more deeply at the most popular movies advertised to teens and note the subject matter and the tone. In almost all of them, teenagers and twenty-somethings are portrayed as self-absorbed partiers and slackers, the last people in the world you want as role models for your children. And reality television? If those groups of people are what is "real" in our world, we are in bigger trouble than we can possibly fathom. The media regularly tell your children that being stupid is funny, that delaying responsibility is admirable, and that the longer they can put off becoming adults the better. So if you allow your teens to watch any movie or TV show they like, know that they have been influenced and inundated by these messages. That just makes your job a whole lot harder.

Problem Parenting Styles and How to Avoid Them

Your work is cut out for you regardless of the media. This is especially true if you find yourself relating to any of the following groups of parents who unknowingly hinder their children from growing up.

Parents Who Pay for Everything

I've taught at some wealthy schools in which parents had the means to pay for everything under the sun. I'm not just talking about middle- and upper-class parents who indulge their children; I'm talking about multimillionaires with private jets and five homes.

Chrystal came from just such a family. Her parents made sure her hair was highlighted every six weeks. She got her nails done every ten days. She wore expensive makeup, clothing, and shoes. She took exotic vacations during school breaks and didn't know what it was like to fly coach. Before she even turned sixteen, she had a brand new BMW waiting for her, delivered with a giant bow. She learned how to drive on that $60,000 car, which she crashed within two weeks of getting her license. So what did her parents do? Why, they purchased her another BMW. When the other students teased her about her poor driving and the fact that her car was immediately—ridiculously—replaced, she breezily responded that she liked the color of the second car better and it had all worked out for the best.

Obviously, Chrystal had zero investment in the car, so she had zero concern when she wrecked it. First, she did nothing to earn it, and since it was one of many expensive gifts she had been given over the years, she had no appreciation for it. Second, when she damaged the car, she had no fear of consequences. Mom and Dad had always ridden in to save the day, and they would do the same this time. It didn't matter that her own poor driving had led to the accident and that she had totaled her first car. Dad's insurance would cover the damages, and her parents would just be happy she was okay. Third, Chrystal knew she would in no way suffer as a result of her carelessness. Another car would be delivered long before any inconvenience, and the problem would be solved for her. To sum up, she had no appreciation, no responsibility, and no consequences. Yet I guarantee you her parents patted themselves on the back for supporting their daughter and providing her with a lush life.

It is not surprising that Chrystal never held a job, had no chores at home, and was rarely held accountable for her academics. If she struggled, tutors were provided immediately. I don't know what happened to Chrystal after she graduated, but I can imagine. What happens to any child who hasn't been taught that every decision has a consequence and that sometimes those consequences hurt?

You may not be as rich or as indulgent as Chrystal's parents, but ask yourself a couple of questions. Have you set a precedent of paying for all your children's wants, without requiring that they do anything to earn their perks and treats? Have you allowed your teenagers to believe that they will graduate college or go out into the workplace and maintain the same lifestyle you have provided for them? Do they have a sense of having to work hard to provide for themselves and a realization that they won't always be able to afford everything they desire? Are they grateful for what they are given, and do they value their possessions? Remember, you don't have to be wealthy to spoil your children. If you haven't taught work ethic and gratitude to your children, they just might be spoiled, regardless of the family income.

Parents Who Treat Their Teenagers Like Children

Parents can do this in any number of ways. Usually, their intentions are to show their love for their children by performing acts of kindness for them. I certainly don't discourage this, but it is important to realize that doing everything for children is actually not loving; it is hurtful and inhibiting to children's sense of self-worth. High school provides four years to slowly relinquish control of your children and to increase the responsibility you expect from them. You will always have opportunities to demonstrate your love for your children, but doing everything for them shouldn't be one of them.

Andre loved his parents, especially his mom, who mothered him thoroughly throughout his high school years. She packed his lunch every day, laundered his clothes whenever he needed them, cleaned his room and made his bed while he was at school, organized his backpack, and kept a calendar of his activities and assignment due dates. Both parents carted him all over town to movies, Friday night skate sessions, friends' homes, wherever he wanted to go. Their schedule was dependent on Andre's schedule, and they were perfectly fine with that. As you can imagine, so was Andre.

What he didn't appreciate, however, was that his parents also treated him like a child in other areas of his life. They spoke to him as if he needed lengthy explanations for every answer. They didn't ask him how he felt about things; they simply told him how to feel based on long-held family beliefs and traditions. They wanted to know who he was with at all times and called his cell phone if they hadn't talked to him in an hour. He had to check in every time he left someone's house and went to a different location, once before he left and once after he arrived safely. If he had any problems at school, his parents involved themselves immediately, insisting on a teacher meeting before Andre could deal with the matter on his own. In short, they were stifling, sometimes out of concern, sometimes because that's how they had always done things, and always because they had not loosened the reins in the years since Andre was a little boy.

I've had students who are expected to check in with their parents throughout the school day. Why? I have no earthly idea. I've been in the middle of a lesson and a student's cell phone has gone off. When I walk over to retrieve the phone, whose name is displayed prominently? MOM. For the life of me, I cannot imagine what parents could possibly need that would require interrupting their children at school. I've seen parents stop everything they were doing to run a forgotten lunch to school for their kids. I've seen them sit in a car pickup line for an hour rather than let their fourteen-year-old board a school bus for the ten-minute drive home. The extent of overprotectiveness is astounding, and kids truly dislike it.

They love the nurturing and they love knowing their parents care, but they hate being treated like children. Make their favorite dinner, take them out for driving lessons, support their social lives, and keep your home open to their friends. But please don't baby them. You are doing them no favors, and you are cheating them out of the experience of growing up and making their own decisions.

Parents Who Don't Prepare Their Kids for the Future

This is the easiest group to fall into because, as you have discovered, time with your children just flies by. It is simplest to do what you have always done, and it takes work to consciously think about and plan change. It's not exactly part of parents' weekly or monthly routine to sit down and reflect on how they are doing as parents, but it should be, especially during these years. I recommend regularly asking yourself what you could be doing to help your children prepare for their futures, when you are no longer around every day to offer guidance.

I conducted a study of over one hundred current and former students and asked them to name one area they feel unprepared to handle as adults. The number one answer by far was finances. Do you know that most high school students have no idea how to write out a check? If their parents have set up bank accounts for them, they couldn't tell you the first thing about those accounts. In other words, they don't know their balance, they don't know if they have been charged any fees, and they don't check their monthly statements. Most do not have their own credit cards, and I get that. Parents are terrified that their kids are going to splurge on major purchases they can't afford, accrue debt, or fail to make payments, resulting in huge interest fees. That is a legitimate concern, but there is a relatively simple solution: educate them fully before turning a credit card over to them. Begin by finding them a card with a low credit limit. Special credit cards exist solely for students and have low limits, extra security against identity theft, and some forgiveness for the first time users forget to pay their balance. Talk to them about how and when to use the card. Treat the entire process like the teachable moment it is, rather than avoiding it.

Do the same thing with checkbooks and debit cards. And don't assume, as I did, that your kids will know the difference between a credit card and a debit card. They don't. Again, teach them when to use each of these cards and when not to. Kids today love to make purchases online, and they will use their debit cards unless you tell them all the reasons why they shouldn't. When they go off to college, most will order their textbooks online. They need to know how to use a credit card responsibly and how to recognize legitimate websites and sellers.

In general, they need to be schooled in good money management. This includes securing their checks, credit card, and debit card in a safe place; reviewing monthly statements for errors; saving and reviewing receipts from purchases; knowing the rules and restrictions for their cards and their bank; understanding how to fill out bank deposit and withdrawal forms; and so on. It means having discussions about the money coming in versus the money going out. When your children turn eighteen and move on to wherever life takes them, they should be fully cognizant of basic financial responsibility.

If you haven't already done so, you must start this process now. If your children work, insist that they put an agreed-upon portion of every paycheck into savings, even if it is only $5. Teach them early and often that they must do this. In our house, we always insisted that money be spent responsibly. Gift money, however, could be used to purchase whatever our children liked, unless a specification had been made by the gift giver. Your children should have the same freedom adults do to enjoy monetary gifts, so give it to them. The key here is to treat them like adults when it comes to finances. Put the responsibility on them to listen and learn from your wisdom, and constantly remind them of the seriousness of good financial management. But also let them enjoy their windfalls. It will teach them that money is a necessity but can also be a joy. They should understand that they must pay for their needs first, put some money away for their futures second, and treat themselves third. Imagine how much better our country's economy would be if everyone taught their children these lessons.

An added bonus is that when you turn some financial responsibility and freedom over to your children, they appreciate your trust and belief in their abilities. They see you treating them as adults and they strive to rise to the occasion.

Talking to Them Like Adults

The same applies to talking to your children with respect, just as you would another adult. In my survey, kids mentioned time and time again that they knew they were growing up when their parents started talking to them like adults.

An emerging-adult dialogue about a common teen issue might sound like this:

Dad: Hey, Melissa, you look like something's on your mind. Do you want to talk about it?

Melissa (hesitating, pretty sure she doesn't want to have this conversation with Dad): Ummm, not really.

Dad: Okay, but you look like something's bothering you, and I'd like to help if I can.

Melissa: Well, if I tell you, do you promise not to get mad?

Dad: I'll try not to, but that's a pretty unfair question. Are you about to tell me that you wrecked my car? Because—I'm just being honest here—that will make me mad.

Melissa (with a smile): No, Dad. But it's pretty serious stuff and it's going to make you uncomfortable.

Dad: So what else is new? Lay it on me.

Melissa (deep breath): Well, some of my friends are getting together on Saturday night at Courtney's house, and they want me to come. I want to, but the last time, a bunch of people were smoking, and then I felt like I had to try it, and now I'm thinking it's probably expected of me, you know?

Dad: When you say "smoking," what exactly do you mean by that?

Melissa: Weed. Pot. Mary Jane. You know.

Dad: Uh-huh. And you tried this. What did you think of it?

Melissa: It wasn't bad, but it wasn't really my thing. Dad, this is making me really uncomfortable. I can't even believe we're talking about this.

Dad: Well, yeah, this kind of conversation isn't really a walk in the park, but I know this stuff goes on, and I know you're exposed to it. I want you to talk to me about it. So you said it wasn't really your thing. You didn't enjoy it?

Melissa: No, not really. I kind of wondered what the point was, to be honest. Everyone else was acting like it was so great, and it didn't really do much for me.

Dad: Well, remember that most people will say it's great just because that's what their friends expect them to say. For a lot of people it's not fun and, as you said, kind of pointless.

Melissa (scrutinizing Dad's face): Have you ever tried it?

Dad (looking Melissa straight in the eyes): Does it matter? You've already recognized that different people have different reactions to drugs, and you don't like it. Other people's use of drugs really shouldn't have any bearing at all on your decisions about them. Not to mention the fact that they're illegal, and getting caught with them could blow your chances for future opportunities.

Melissa: So you're not going to tell me? That must mean that you tried it.

Dad (chuckling): Believe what you will. The point is, again, that it doesn't matter at all. What matters is *your* decision and the consequences you may face as a result of that decision. Think long and hard about this, and whatever you do, don't let your friends' poor decisions affect what you decide. You are your own person and will be confronted with this sort of thing countless times in the future. Now is as good a time as any to evaluate where you stand and who you are.

Melissa: So what do I do if I go to Courtney's and someone hands me a joint and waits to see what I'll do? Because that will happen.

Dad: Just shake your head and tell them the truth—that you don't really like it and are going to take a pass. Or better yet, avoid going places where you know this kind of thing is taking place.

Melissa (rolling her eyes): Oh, Dad . . .

Dad: Please hear me out (waits for Melissa to give him her attention again). First of all, where are Courtney's parents when this is going on? Do you realize that if you and your friends are caught, her parents will face terrible scrutiny, legal action, fines, and the negative publicity that comes from things like this? If they know this is going on, shame on them. They need to seriously work on their parenting skills. If they don't, I feel horrible for them that their child and her friends are betraying their trust.

Melissa: They know and they don't really care. They just ignore it, or pretend it's not happening or something.

Dad: Well, that's incredibly sad and irresponsible of them, and I don't really want you there if the parents aren't going to be parents. So why don't you invite your friends over here as much as possible? Make this the go-to home. We won't hover over you, but we won't let you smoke pot either. Let us be the bad guys. And when you're not here, my best advice is to just be honest with your friends. They're your friends, after all. You should be able to be honest with them.

Melissa: I'll think about it.

Dad: Sounds good. I know you're sick of hearing this, but remember that you always have options. Never feel that you have to give in and do something you don't want to do. You can always call us to pick you up, you can always make us the bad guy, and you can always be honest with your friends. You're smart enough to know there will always be consequences, and you should think about them before you make any decisions.

What didn't happen in this conversation is as important as what did:

- Dad didn't react to Melissa's confession with shock and immediate disapproval. He took it in stride, even if it was killing him inside, because he knew if he overreacted, Melissa wouldn't open up to him again.

- Dad didn't treat Melissa like a child or show a lack of respect for her as a thinking human being. He didn't reprimand her, scream at her, tell her she had done a stupid thing, or ask her if she had any sense in her head. He wasn't sarcastic and he didn't lecture tirelessly.

- Dad teased gently and instilled some humor where he could to lighten the mood and make the conversation more comfortable.

- When Melissa confessed she had tried pot, he didn't try to shame her or tell her how disappointed he was in her.

- When Melissa asked Dad if he had ever smoked pot, he didn't give her any ammunition to continue with her negative behaviors. As parents, you are under no obligation to reveal your secrets or your past mistakes to your children. Notice that he didn't lie; he just chose not to answer. And what good would it have done if he had? If he had never smoked pot, Melissa might have discounted his opinion as uninformed. If he had, Melissa might have justified her behavior and taken the attitude that "everyone does it, even my dad."

- Dad played the role of a responsible parent. He remembered that his daughter is still in the stage between childhood and adulthood and, therefore, not an adult yet. So he used his parental influence to tell her he doesn't want her going to an unsupervised home, but he also offered her viable alternatives such as meeting at their home.

- Melissa was given an easy out with her friends: My parents won't let me. This is a comfort to a number of kids out there who want to do the right thing but aren't strong or mature enough yet to stand up on their own. If they can place the blame on their parents it lets them off the hook, and even if they never tell you this, they appreciate it.

- Dad did not demand or insist or lay down the law in any type of punitive way. Instead he suggested options and helped Melissa think through them. He reminded her that she always has the freedom of choice. Had he punished her for being honest with him and asking for advice, that would be the last time she talked to him about anything important.

- Dad acknowledged that this would be the first of many temptations Melissa will face in the next few years. He guided her through a critical thinking process she can utilize any time a choice like this comes up. Because she is being taught to use reason and good judgment in her life decisions, Melissa won't be as likely to repeat mindless, caught-in-the-moment behavior. She won't be one of the many teenagers who escape their parents' clutches and then immediately go crazy in college or out in the real world.

- Dad never told Melissa she couldn't hang out with her friends anymore. This would have been lethal to the parent-teenager relationship. Avoid—at all costs— choosing friends for your kids or denying them friend- ships with kids of their choosing. For one thing, they are just a couple of years away from legal adulthood and need to learn how to make personal decisions without constant direction from Mom and Dad. For another, no matter how hard you try, you cannot control who your children befriend. Stop trying. You will only alienate your children from you and cause them to lie and sneak around behind your back. I guarantee this.

Your goal during these years is to transition from making decisions for your kids to guiding them through good decision-making skills until, eventually, they can do this on their own. The dialogue I have provided is fairly generic, and that's on purpose. You can adapt it to fit any number of situations. And, of course, you should personalize your approach. If you have strong religious convictions, those should form the foundation of your discussions about controversial issues. If you have personal stories from your own life, family members, or friends, you should include those. But the two tenets that should remain the same regardless of the topic or your own personal spin on it is a respectful exchange of ideas and the understanding that choices lead to consequences. You may still dole out consequences of your own during these years, but your children should learn that life will deal them plenty of repercussions when you are not around to do so. Let them accept those ramifications like the adults they are learning to become.

My daughter recently reminded me of an incident that happened in her late teens, a time she described as "feeling like a true adult." She had been driving to a summer job when she found herself in a speed trap. She, along with a string of cars all going over the speed limit, was pulled over and issued a ticket. A $200 ticket. She called me through tears, terrified that I would be angry, embarrassed to admit she had deserved the ticket, and worried that her dad and I would discipline her in some way. She said she was never so relieved as she was when she heard my reaction.

"Oh, Rachel, that's terrible. Were you really speeding?"

"Yes," she replied. "By about fifteen miles per hour. It was in that one spot—you know the one—and apparently the speed limit is only thirty-five miles per hour there. That's why they were pulling everyone over."

"Geez. I've been caught in those speed traps before and they are terrible. I'm so sorry this happened to you. I know how upsetting that is."

Rachel said the relief she felt at that moment was palpable. She knew without a shadow of a doubt that we wouldn't pay the ticket for her and that that one ticket would cost her a week's salary from her summer job. Those were life's consequences, and she knew we wouldn't save her from them. But she also knew we supported her and loved her and felt her pain.

"That's how I knew I was really an adult," she explained. "I knew you would always be there for me, but I also knew that I was on my own when it came to dealing with the consequences of my decisions. As bad as that ticket was, I felt great."

It didn't take much on my part to make this happen. I just put myself in her place—just as I would do for a friend or anyone else I respected—and offered support. I knew the consequences and the lesson were already there, and that allowed me to play the role of empathetic parent.

Final Suggestions for Preparing Kids for Adulthood

If you haven't begun to move in this direction, now is the time. Consider what I have discussed in this chapter, and consider the following thirteen suggestions for how to prepare your children for adulthood:

1. Make it clear—always—that when they graduate high school, they are expected to get a job, pursue their life plan, or go to college. Do not allow your children to "flake" or "veg" or any other slang expression that means pure dependency on Mom and Dad. Do not let them take a year off to relax or figure out what they want to do. They can think while they are working. They can think while they're taking classes. But not a lot of thinking is going to happen while they are watching TV and texting their friends.

2. Let them know that they will not live with you after college graduation, except to help them get on their feet. It's one thing to allow a new graduate to live at home for a year or two if they are employed and saving for their own place. It is another to let them live at home and do nothing. And it's not acceptable for them to be gainfully employed and spending all their money on toys, with no deadline in place for them to set out on their own. Their plans should be reasonable and affordable; they should not live at home for five years so they can afford to buy a four-bedroom home. And please make it clear that

once they are gone, they're gone. Of course, you will always be there in an emergency if they need you, but the expectation should be that they won't.

3. Kids don't need master's degrees, and many, many kids get them just to delay entering the work world. I have always contended that no one should get an advanced degree unless and until they have spent time working in the field. They have to determine, first and foremost, if they even like the field before they invest more time and money into textbook learning. In addition, advanced degrees should be funded by the adults who are pursuing them, or the companies for whom they work, not Mom and Dad.

4. If college is in your teenagers' futures, allot a certain amount of money (whatever you can reasonably afford or feel comfortable paying) for tuition; if they go over that amount, they are responsible for the difference. Again, where they go to college is entirely their choice. If they choose an out-of-state university, they will pay out-of-state tuition. If they take longer than four years to earn their degree, they should pay for the fifth year. If they live beyond their means, they should feel the financial pinch when the money runs out.

5. Give them increasing responsibilities in every area you can think of. Let them go to the doctor themselves and learn about insurance and copays. Let them use their phone's navigational system to find their destination rather than writing out directions for them. Insist that they keep a calendar and take responsibility for remembering and reminding you of their weekly activities.

6. Celebrate milestones as important, happy steps to growing up. Passing their driving test, learning how to mow the lawn, earning their first paycheck, opening up a new savings account—these are all steps to adulthood that should be celebrated. As hard as it may be, try not to cry and hug them and tell them they'll always be your babies when they are standing there holding their freshly laminated driver's license. I have seen this happen, and it is uncomfortable for children and sends the message that growing up is negative and hurts their parents. Sure, you can cry a little when you drop them off at college, but make sure they know they are tears of joy and pride. Never make your kids feel guilty for growing up.

7. Respect their decisions and steps toward independence, even if they choose differently than you would. They will love and appreciate the respect you show them and extend the same to you.

8. Insist that your teens do summer work. This can include anything from weekend babysitting to forty-hour-a-week jobs. Throughout high school, they should make their own spending money and put some away for their futures. If at all financially possible, avoid having your children work during the school year. Always stress that school is their job and first priority ten months out of the year. If they must work an outside job, have them work the minimum number of hours so they can keep school as their central focus. This will teach them to prioritize in the future.

9. Teach children that every type of lifestyle comes at a price. If they want more "treats," they will have to

work harder, save more, and keep learning. Do not provide a lifestyle for your kids that they have not in any way contributed to or sacrificed for.

10. Have your kids take ownership of their education, both now and in the future. For instance, if they are going to college, they should select the college. Give feedback and talk about areas for consideration, but put the onus on them to research colleges and plan college visits before they make the ultimate decision. Believe me, if they aren't invested in the decision they won't be invested in the education.

11. Increase your level of trust in them. Do not make them text you every time they leave one place and arrive at another. Do not expect them to check in constantly or seek your advice before they make every little decision.

12. Speak to teenagers as adults, like you trust them to handle most of whatever comes up from day to day. Don't ask them if they're okay and baby them over incidents they should be able to handle.

13. Treat boys and girls evenhandedly. There is no reason to extend permissions to a boy that you would not extend to a girl, and vice versa. Always parent the individual child; do not cater to traditional gender roles. Brothers and sisters are acutely aware of sexist and unfair decision making on your part.

CAVEAT

All kids are unique. Trust your judgment when it comes to how much freedom and responsibility to extend to your children. Don't compare kids within the same family, and avoid comparing your children to others. Your goal should be to increase your trust and expectations accordingly for each child while avoiding comparing that child's milestones to others'. It makes no difference if his sister could be trusted at sixteen and he can't. What matters is what you are doing now to make sure he can be trusted at seventeen.

All We Can Do Is Our Best

I COVERED A LOT OF TERRITORY IN THIS BOOK, AND HOPE-
fully you discovered some new insights into your teenagers
and the best ways to communicate with them. I would like to
leave you with some final thoughts to reflect on as you consider
how to move forward with your parenting.

First, the earlier you can start incorporating these ideas the
better. I've spoken with parents of very young children who are
eager for this advice right now. They are correct in their assumption that the teenage years will run much more smoothly if parents incorporate this methodology at a young age. Surely, the
earlier you begin to build a strong parenting foundation, the
easier the "difficult teenage years" will be. So although I have
directed these words toward parents of teenagers, many of the
ideas and concepts can be applied to younger children. If you set
a tone of mutual respect and ownership of one's choices when
your children are younger, they will more likely accept it as "the
way we do things in our house."

And speaking of the way to do things, remember that being
fair with the children in your family does not mean parenting
them in the exact same way. What works beautifully for one
child may be a tough sell for another. Strive to understand what
motivates each of your children as individuals, and differentiate

your parenting accordingly. But be careful to be equitable when doling out ice cream and punishments and to be evenhanded in your reactions to their behavior. Kids notice when their siblings' actions are quickly forgiven but their own are relentlessly punished. Be fair in sharing the same amount of love balanced with discipline. But you may need to love and discipline each child differently. Fair parenting doesn't mean identical parenting.

While you are determining what works with your children, you will have to tweak and refine your approach. My insights and advice serve as solid starting points, and you will see success with these methods. But every child is unique, as you well know, so you will need to test the waters, note the reactions, and adjust. You will need to broach a sensitive topic carefully, monitor your child's willingness to open up, and modify accordingly. Parenting is not an exact science; it is an art. There are nuances, gray areas—some would argue minefields—that you must tiptoe through on your way to parenting success. What I have provided are avenues that will lead to shared respect, increased responsibility and self-reliance, and promotion of critical thinking and self-reflection. Some children will adopt these habits with little effort on your part; others will exhaust you and make you work tirelessly for your parenting gold star.

Remember, though, that you have allies in your children's teachers. Work cooperatively with them and create partnerships with the mission of doing what is best for your children. Most teachers have good intentions and choose education because they genuinely like working with children. They are like me in that they have seen just about everything, and they are valuable resources in helping you recognize all facets of your children's personalities and work habits. Listen to them. Ask them direct questions that will help you help your children. It is crucial that your children see their parents and their teachers working together in relationships that exude cooperation and a shared desire for their success.

Finally, concentrate on behaviors and situations that are important, let the unimportant go, and remind yourself constantly that all you can do is the best you can do. Hopefully, this book has helped you uncover ways to raise quality individuals who know how to properly interact with various people in a plethora of situations. If I have heightened your awareness, shed some light on the adolescent mind, given you permission to stand outside the crowd, or helped in just one area, I've done my job.

NOTES

CHAPTER 1: How to Motivate Your Kids

1. B. F. Skinner, *The Behavior of Organisms* (New York: Appleton-Century-Crofts, 1991): 20–21, 40, 112.
2. A. H. Maslow, "A Theory of Human Motivation," *Psychological Review* 50, no. 4 (1943): 370–396.
3. A. Bandura, D. Ross, and S. A. Ross, "Transmission of Aggression Through the Imitation of Aggressive Models," *Journal of Abnormal and Social Psychology* 63, 575–582.
4. Joseph Ferrari, "Psychology of Procrastination: Why People Put Off Important Tasks Until the Last Minute," American Psychological Association, April 5, 2010, http://www.apa.org/news/press/releases/2010/04/procrastination.aspx, accessed November 18, 2013.

CHAPTER 3: Too Old to Run to Mom or Dad: When to Get Involved and When to Step Back

1. Bill & Melinda Gates Foundation, "Primary Sources: 2012: America's Teachers on the Teaching Profession" (Scholastic, 2012), p. 12, http://www.scholastic.com/primarysources/pdfs/Gates2012_full.pdf, accessed May 21, 2014.
2. Foster Cline and Jim Fay, *Parenting with Love and Logic: Teaching Children Responsibility* (Colorado Springs, CO: Pinon, 1990): 23–25.

CHAPTER 4: Getting Teens to Accept Responsibility for Their Work, Their Decisions, and Their Mistakes

1. Susan Whitbourne, "Excuses, Excuses, Excuses: Why People Lie, Cheat, and Procrastinate," *Psychologytoday.com*, May 18, 2010, http://www.psychologytoday.com/blog/fulfillment-any-age /201005/excuses-excuses-excuses-why-people-lie-cheat-and-procrastinate, accessed August 15, 2013.

CHAPTER 8: College Isn't for Everyone: Is It Best for *Your* Child?

1. Mike Bowler, "Dropouts Loom Large for Schools," *U.S. News & World Report*, August 19, 2009, http://www.usnews.com/educa tion/articles/2009/08/19/dropouts-loom-large-for-schools, accessed November 18, 2013.

2. Daniel De Vise, "Many Students Could Skip Remedial Classes, Studies Find," *Washington Post*, February 28, 2012, http://www. washingtonpost.com/blogs/college-inc/post/many-students-could-skip-remedial-classes-studies-find/2012/02/28/gIQA5p5rgR_blog .html, accessed December 4, 2013.

3. Susan Adams, "Half of College Grads Are Working Jobs That Don't Require a Degree," *Forbes*, May 28, 2013, http://www.forbes.com/ sites/susanadams/2013/05/28/half-of-college-grads-are-working-jobs-that-dont-require-a-degree/, accessed December 3, 2013.

4. Bill Symonds, "Report Calls for National Effort to Get Millions of Young Americans onto a Realistic Path to Employability," *Ed. The Magazine of the Harvard Graduate School of Education*, Summer 2011, http://www.gse.havard.edu/news-impact/2011/02 /report-calls-for-national-effort-to-get-millions-of-young-americans-onto-a-realistic-path-to-employa/, accessed December 4, 2013.

5. Harvard Graduate School of Education, *Pathways to Prosperity*, February 2011, p. 10.

6. Cecilia Capuzzi Simon, "Major Decisions," *New York Times*, November 4, 2012, "Education Life," 13.

CHAPTER 10: Making Sure Teens Know That the Way They Look and Sound Matters

1. Carol Kinsey Goman, "Seven Seconds to Make a First Impression," *Forbes*, February 13, 2011, http://www.forbes.com/sites/carolkinseygoman/2011/02/13/seven-seconds-to-make-a-first-impression/, accessed December 4, 2013.
2. Lauren Bayne Anderson, "Could a New 'Social Media Background Check' Cost You the Job?," *MonsterCollege*, July 27, 2011, http://college.monster.com/news/articles/2145-could-a-new-social-media-background-check-cost-you-the-job, accessed December 4, 2013.

CHAPTER 12: How to Prepare Your Teens for Adulthood

1. Richard Fry, "A Rising Share of Young Adults Live in Their Parents' Home," Pew Research Center, August 1, 2013, http://www.pewsocialtrends.org/2013/08/01/a-rising-share-of-young-adults-live-in-their-parents-home, accessed May 21, 2014.

INDEX

ABOUT THE AUTHOR

REBECCA DEURLEIN is a veteran high school teacher with a doctorate in education and the experience of raising two kids of her own. Her areas of expertise include understanding and correcting behavior issues, differentiating for learners, motivating children to higher levels of critical thinking, and encouraging kids to challenge themselves.

Rebecca is a seasoned public speaker who shares a combination of humorous personal experiences, educational research, and down-to-earth practical advice to inform parents on teen issues. She is equally comfortable speaking with small, interactive groups of parents as she is addressing an arena of 5,000. Rebecca is an active member of Rotary International and serves on the Board of Directors for Achieve Fort Bend, a dropout prevention program focused on fostering teen motivation and career exploration.

Rebecca lives in Houston, Texas, and teaches English at Fort Bend Christian Academy. She formerly taught in the Naperville Public School System, outside of Chicago, IL; the Forsyth County School System in Atlanta, GA; and the Roanoke Public School System in Roanoke, VA. She owns a freelance writing business and in her spare time, she enjoys kickboxing and yoga.

For more information about Rebecca's writing work and speaking engagements, visit her website at www.rebeccadeurlein.com.